Measure Up

MEASURE UP

Mastering Your Career Search Like a Boss

Josh McAfee & Trisha Garek Harp

NEW YORK

LONDON • NASHVILLE • MELBOURNE • VANCOUVER

Measure Up

Mastering Your Career Search Like a Boss

© 2021 Josh McAfee and Trisha Garek Harp

Published in New York, New York, by Morgan James Publishing. Morgan James is a trademark of Morgan James, LLC. www.MorganJamesPublishing.com

Proudly distributed by Ingram Publisher Services.

Morgan James BOGO™

A **FREE** ebook edition is available for you or a friend with the purchase of this print book.

CLEARLY SIGN YOUR NAME ABOVE

Instructions to claim your free ebook edition:
1. Visit MorganJamesBOGO.com
2. Sign your name CLEARLY in the space above
3. Complete the form and submit a photo of this entire page
4. You or your friend can download the ebook to your preferred device

ISBN 9781631953033 paperback
ISBN 9781631953040 eBook
Library of Congress Control Number:
2020944080

Cover Design by:
Christopher Kirk
www.GFSstudio.com

Interior Design by:
Chris Treccani
www.3dogcreative.net

Morgan James is a proud partner of Habitat for Humanity Peninsula and Greater Williamsburg. Partners in building since 2006.

Get involved today! Visit MorganJamesPublishing.com/giving-back

To my wife, Kerri; our daughter, Lana, who as of writing this will be born in 3 weeks; to everyone who pushed me to write this book and encouraged me along the way; and to God for blessing me with a career and life that's revolved around helping and been so fulfilling. Thank you so much for everything you have done to support, encourage, and challenge me. — Josh

I would like to dedicate this book to all of my past coworkers who have felt stuck and trapped in their jobs. You are not stuck. You always have options. I'm really proud to put many of our conversations to good use through this book. —Trisha

TABLE OF CONTENTS

Thank you for purchasing "Measure UP".
We developed a free "Get Started Today"
download to compliment this book which will
guide you through the high level steps of
our process. To download the guide, visit
CareerWhisperer.co/MeasureUpToday

PREFACE

It's amazing what can happen over a simple cup of coffee. Over two years ago, we met at a networking event unsure of what to expect but knowing we needed to collaborate on this book.

It was 2018. Josh had more than 25 years in recruiting and career coaching and had recently sold the recruiting business he started in 2001 in which he'd worked with and coached thousands of people in career transition. He'd been keeping track of what people were doing really well—and what they were doing poorly—in their career search. Colleagues and friends coaxed him to start writing a book.

Trish, meanwhile, had followed two different career paths: Working with adults with developmental disabilities and working with entrepreneurs and their significant others. Josh and his wife, Kerri, were her clients. As Trish progressed more into the coaching realm, she realized that much of her psychological teachings could be applied to people in search of a more fulfilling career path.

So there we were, sipping our coffee of choice, when we decided we'd write a book together. It would be a way to give back to people and communities who'd been helpful to us, and also to do a little good in the world. We'd teach readers on communication, recognizing strengths and weaknesses, and figuring it out how to present themselves in a way that would highlight their value and resonate with others. We felt we both had some pretty powerful concepts to share with you.

Why now? For one, the material in this book will always be relevant. The technology will change, and the way people are interviewed will change, but these principles are timeless. It's about the ability to be genuine and focused on how you're valuable, why you're valuable, instead of focusing on the things you want, feel, think, and need.

When you've read this book, you'll discover our words will carry over to all aspects of your life in the way you choose to interact, find your network, and exist in the world as a whole. There's a better way to present yourself, a better way to communicate, a better way to identify and target who you want to be around instead of just being around who's around. With a little effort and intentionality, this will be not just a shift in your career, but also a shift in your life.

Think of your career this way. You're in the most amazing movie of your life. This is your adventure. Who do you want to be? You get to choose based on who you discover you are.

Let our adventure together begin.

INTRODUCTION

Rex was a support engineer fixing the bugs in systems and helping customers with their technical problems. He was really good at it—so good that his company came to rely on him a little too much. Insisting they needed Rex in this role, his boss kept him there for three years. Feeling as if he were slowly boiling in a lobster pot, Rex had to escape, but didn't know how. Eventually, he updated his resume, posted it on a job board, and applied to several new positions.

Role vs. Value

Rex received lots of interest as a support engineer but no interest in any of the more technical roles he was ready to grow into. This left him feeling even more trapped and a little depressed. Why couldn't anyone see his value? Why wasn't anyone interested? He went back to work for another 6 months with the water around him slowly getting hotter and hotter. Josh, who had a client looking for a technical support engineer, found Rex's resume and called him. As they talked, it was obvious that to Rex, this was another interview for a role he really didn't want. After about 10 minutes, Josh stopped and asked Rex how he thought this interview was going. "Terribly," said Rex. He was a little taken aback but humbly repeated, "terribly". Josh asked him what was going on and shared that he could "feel" his frustration over the phone. What came out of Rex next was 3.5 years of frustration, anger, pain, anxiety, and helplessness.

"What are you really good at?" Josh asked Rex, who said he was great at understanding customers' problems. He was also really good at finding hacks to meet their needs; and he loved working with the development team to solve common issues. Josh asked Rex if he'd like to move into a developer or programmer role where he could have a bigger impact. Over the phone, Rex started to choke up and said, "Yes!" He explained how he didn't get anything other than support jobs from "all" of his efforts. Josh laughed, telling Rex he was a mislabeled product. By going "shopping" in the support engineer aisle, Josh had found Rex. But in what aisle did he really belong? "Software developer," Rex answered, his voice brightening as we discussed where he was stuck, what he should be doing differently, and how to apply a few simple principles to his job search.

During the next 8 years, Rex moved into programming jobs with two different companies, earning promotions. Then his original "lobster pot" company asked him to return in a senior development, client-facing role, working directly with the product management team. It was his dream job. But it took so long to land it because Rex was focused on describing his current role instead of his own strengths and value. Throughout this book, we are going to explore how you can do the same, and much more.

Why Are You Here?

- Do you feel disrespected, undervalued—or simply joy-less—at work?
- Were you laid off or fired from your job?
- Is your current work situation lacking security or stability?
- Did you recently get hit with some big expenses, and you realize how much you want to find a better-paying, better-fitting, more rewarding job?

- Do you feel like you've just been going around in circles career-wise for way too long, and it's time to leap into something better?
- Are you recently out of school, and you don't want to waste any time finding a great fit with a great future?
- Do you want to find a job that's more fulfilling, more satisfying, and more financially rewarding than you've ever had?
- Is there just a voice inside saying, "It's time!"?
- Or is your soul simply crying out to you, screaming, "Enough is enough! I need to make some changes!"

If you said "Yes" to any of these questions, you've come to the right place. Turns out that the "crap" has to start hitting the fan pretty hard before people can get themselves energized and motivated enough to go for a job or career change. It's a big deal to step off your familiar career path, take a risk, and put in the effort to find a new home for your job or career.

What This Book Is About

Let's be honest, if you're looking for a job, you're in a highly competitive race for a position, and you don't even know where or what the finish line is. There are a lot of people—hundreds? thousands?—blasting out resumes to the same companies and the same hiring managers that you're hoping to interview with. Given how much competition there is for the best jobs, there are two critically important questions you have to ask yourself:

Question #1: Do you have to compromise yourself, your identity, or your comfort zone just to "fit in" to a great job to be a success, or is there a place you can be true to yourself and still land a great job that reflects your values and nurtures your future?

The answer? No! You do not need to shave off your square edges to fit into someone else's round hole to get hired. In fact, it's exactly the opposite. You just have to seek and find the square hole opportunities that are out there. As unlikely as it may seem, the real silver bullet to finding and landing a super job for yourself is identifying what you are best at doing and then determining where, how, when, and by whom it's most valuable.

And that's what this book is all about. You don't have to trade in your soul to be successful. You can be fully you—but first you have to know who that is, who you want to become, and how to measure up to what you are capable of. We'll show you how to do that. Welcome to the deep end of the pool.

Question #2: If everyone's using the same set of tools, the same strategies, and has the same expectations, how can you set yourself apart so you don't just land a job—you find a position that allows you to contribute, be productive, feel good about yourself, grow, and be rewarded for it, too?

Answer: Read this book. Within these pages, you'll find exceptional strategies, insider perspectives, tactics to use online tools to your advantage, and easy communication templates that are attuned to the current social and technological realities. Whether you're networking and interviewing in the virtual world or the real world, you'll discover how to present your best self. You'll learn how to discover lucrative job prospects before anybody else does. And you'll be given a variety of tools and exercises that build your confidence and help you understand, appreciate, and "sell" your true value in the job marketplace. Finally, you'll learn the most important keys to mastering your interviews, regardless of your history or your personality type.

Sound good? Well, there's more. You'll learn:

- How to be your best self and most attractive as a candidate in an interview and while networking

- How to see yourself as a valuable product in your industry
- How to have and build confidence
- How to leverage your successes and failures for your future
- How to build your value story
- How to reframe your failures and resume gaps to your advantage
- How to turn an interview into a valuable conversation
- How to see yourself through a hiring manager's eyes
- How to build rapport with people
- How to make it easy for someone to hire you
- What to do with your emotional baggage
- How to understand how your skills best match a company's needs
- How to benefit from peer feedback
- How to be seen as someone who wants to contribute
- How to connect with people who can further your career goals and help you locate open positions
- How to build your network, your reputation, and your goodwill

- How to successfully meet with people to connect you to new opportunities
- How to empower yourself, avoid distractions, and work smart to find your job
- How to present yourself professionally while still being true to yourself
- The incredibly important role of a cup of coffee

This is more than just another How-To book; it goes much deeper than that. It is a book that helps you sculpt a personal process that can transform your professional life from the inside out. It will help you manage your career through change—whether it's your choice to change or not.

Let's be clear. This takes work. There is no easy magic formula for you to find a job—a great job, that is—without putting in the time and effort. There are going to be some challenges and situations that will scare the crap out of you and make you want to quit. There will also be things that happen, people you meet, discoveries about yourself, and more, that will be absolutely amazing. But you will have to stretch. If you don't stretch yourself, then you won't learn anything valuable, obtain new skills, expand your network, or evolve into the person you want to be, doing the job you want to do. It's all part of your unique adventure and special story. Your process will require as much time as you can give it, but it will pay off with compounded returns. After all, the game's not over until you win.

Finally, as you proceed on your career adventure, do yourself a favor and remember one important truth: your career isn't who you are—it's what you do in support of who you are. With our expert guidance, you'll gain a greater appreciation for who you are and more confidently, more authentically, and more powerfully find and respond to the career opportunities that lie before you.

CHAPTER 1:

Change Your Mind

If you spend your life looking for the ideal job or a career to come to you, you might as well spend every penny you have on the Powerball Lottery—with a 1 in 292 million chance of winning.

Your job, your career—your new life—is out there. But before you do anything else, let's look at how you harness and use your motivation to find it. This will be a deciding factor in making the odds work *for* you rather than *against y*ou. We know you're fired up, and we are, too.

So what stands in the way? Every one of us has outer situations and people potentially blocking the lives we imagine. And every one of us also has inner motivations for creating the careers and relationships we've always wanted. You can't always control the situation, but you *can* control your thoughts and reactions, not only to the job marketplace but also to the pace of current events.

Reacting to your situation—may seem like the normal and natural thing to do. This was especially true in the ebb and flow of the COVID-19 pandemic, which had almost all of us running for cover—not only because of shelter-in-place restrictions but also because most of our jobs, careers, finances, and security were threatened, or worse.

You might have feelings of fear, anxiety, or anger and you're well-justified to have those feelings. But reacting—or what we call "running from" a problem situation—just isn't going to get you where you want to go. It might get you away from where you are now. But it doesn't necessarily mean that you will end up somewhere you want to be.

You know the fight-or-flight phenomenon that happens anytime we get scared or panicked? Well, when this kicks in, our bodies increase blood flow to our muscles, giving us super-human strength and super-speedy reaction times to help us defeat or outrun our supposed attacker. But that redirection of blood flow starves the brain of the blood and oxygen we need to be at our best.

Typically, we'd advise you to stop your job search when you're afraid because that fear can cause you to react negatively. But it's a new world of uncertainty, and that fear likely won't go away quickly. Now we advise you to shift from reactive mode into creative mode. You can move forward with fear, but deliberately, so you don't make choices or take actions rooted in that fear.

In reactive mode, you operate from a position of weakness instead of strength. You might do poorly in an interview for a great role or accept a job too quickly, with the pressure of mortgage payments and healthcare coverage. You're not taking the time to see the bigger picture and the choices that are in your best interest. You're not preparing a strategy to discover where you can add the most value and what is the best fit for you. A new position can allow you to contribute to others, grow at what you do, and put your purpose in this life to work. But in reactive mode, you're ultimately letting external forces decide your career path. Why not allow your valuable experience, abilities, and talents decide your career path instead?

In this chapter, we're going to show you how to shift your focus—how to change your mind. Instead of defaulting to being *reactive* to your situation, like we're programmed to do, you'll learn how to be *proactive* with your career goals to achieve better results. Instead of running from what isn't working for you, you'll be able to move toward career goals and opportunities that fire you up.

This first step—shifting from reactive mode to the more proactive creative mode—can be one of the most freeing and impactful things you can do in your journey to create a new career path.

Awareness is Power

Working toward your career goals includes focusing on how you can add the most value in the world rather than only what feels good, fun, or easy. This will lead to experiences that light you up when you think and talk about them. You'll find fulfillment in knowing you've brought value to others and you've built relationships with the people with whom you've accomplished amazing things. When you work proactively instead of just reacting to life, you ultimately get to become what you are capable of becoming. The investment you put into it can help you create a life where you blossom rather than wither like a plant in poor soil with no water.

Because your reactive emotions and motivations can ultimately derail your career search, it's time to learn ways to manage them. You will almost assuredly experience fear and uncertainty during your search, but you can reduce their impact and move forward more effectively.

Angie's Story

During the recession of 2008–2009, Josh was at a gathering with about 50 technology recruiters. A woman we'll call Angie walked in the room and proceeded to shake each recruiter's hand with the same introduction: "Hi, my name's Angie. I just graduated from Georgia State, and I want to be a graphic designer."

It was just unbelievable gumption, Josh thought, and she was very, very proactive with what she was doing—very intentional. She was savvy enough to find a room of 50 technology recruiters and tell all of them that she was looking for a job. And everyone else was watching her as well, just in complete awe of her proactive confidence.

She ended up getting an offer from one of Josh's clients and four offers from two other recruiters in the room as well. It was absolutely brilliant.

Exercise: Taking Inventory

To get started, set some time aside to take an inventory of what's holding you back from a new job or career. Are you too loyal to your boss? Too tied up in marriage concerns to focus on networking? Grab a notebook, or type on your computer—choose whatever method of writing best suits you. Spend a couple of days becoming aware of the overpowering fears and obstacles you face in your current work and personal life. By doing so, you will have already shifted to creative thinking, becoming proactive in this way, able to acknowledge your thoughts and feelings more easily. Writing down your fears, issues, and concerns will put you in a better place to respond differently. You'll be in a stronger position to shift into a more positive mindset. It'll be easier to refocus your awareness on how you want your mind and body to respond and to keep your focus on the positive outcomes you want to create. You'll be freed up to take action on building the career or finding the job that truly fulfills you.

Awareness is power; it is a skill to be learned and honed. In the immortal words of Michael Jackson, there's power in starting with "the man in the mirror" when looking to make a change. Awareness of what might spiral you into self-pity or lack of sleep and how you react is an important first step to making that change. So be brave enough to look at yourself and make a change in your awareness and responses.

Your Shift to Creative Thinking

Now that you have your inventory, it's time to make the shift into the right mindset for making those odds work for you instead of against you. We'll get your mind to stop racing from those terrible thoughts about change. We'll help you prepare a list of accomplishments. And then it's time to really start measuring up to make the change.

Exercise: Worst-Case Scenario

One reason many people get stuck in reaction mode is that they naturally let their minds run to worst-case scenarios when confronted with triggers.

Their boss is toxic, and they fear they'll get fired for no good reason. They'll be unable to find a replacement job to feed their family. They run to worst-case scenarios that only take into account part of the problem. When they get into worst-case scenario thinking, emotions generally run high. Even worse, they stop considering their possibilities when they hit the worst-case scenario. In this example, they stop planning when they get fired. So, in their mind, they believe unemployment is their ultimate result, essentially deciding their future *will* be unemployment and despair if they don't find a different job—any job—quickly.

To help you avoid this outcome, we want you to do an objective worst-case scenario for you and your career. And if your thinking leads to something negative, keep going.

Ask yourself, what terrible future is your mind or heart telling you might happen if you stay in your current situation? What if you shift to creative thinking and find a different job? What exactly are you afraid of? If something negative happens, what can you do to improve your situation?

Play your own game, identifying your potential Worst-Case scenario. Will your salary plummet? Will your spouse leave you? Will you have to learn an entirely new set of skills? Write down your worst fears so you can see them in black and white, which reduces their power. Then think of at least three ways you would improve your situation if your worst fears came true—which is, we remind you, very unlikely. If you're in a relationship, and your worst-case scenario impacts your partner, play the "game" with them once you've completed your initial list.

Exercise: Personal & Professional Accomplishments

Next, write down your professional and personal accomplishments and successes. Did you lead a team in sales? Was there a time you brought smiles to peoples' faces with your competence and kindness? Maybe your creative ideas helped initiate a new solution for a certain market segment. Perhaps you created a presentation that helped your company and its clients gain a deeper understanding of their performance metrics. Have you ever won an award, been recognized for an accomplishment or had someone in your life share how you brought value to them or the company? Have you done volunteer work that's had a positive impact on the community?

As you move through your job search journey, keep your list of accomplishments handy to remind you that what you set out to do, you *can* do. Take a glance at your accomplishments when your fears start to appear. Let them be a reminder that you have been valuable in a variety of arenas, and that you will do so again—with greater impact and greater success than ever before. We'll also refer to this list later on as you learn how to place yourself effectively within the marketplace.

Exercise: Find the Fire in Your Belly

Trisha's dad used to say that he had a fire in his belly around his career. For him, that fire was a strong desire to achieve greatness. He was a real estate entrepreneur, and in the bathroom he kept a framed Paul Palnik cartoon showing a man yelling out a window of a high-rise apartment. With fists pumping the air, the man was shouting, "SOMEDAY I'M GONNA OWN THIS TOWN!" She loved that little drawing—not only for the way it made her feel about her dad and his sense of himself, but also because it inspired her to want to "own HER own town" and do what she loves.

How strong is that fire in your belly? How badly do you want to reach your goals? What are you willing to do or sacrifice to achieve your dreams? What is motivating you from deep within to pursue a satisfying, new job or career? Plan a break from your job search process to take account of what's guiding you at the deepest level of your core. What is urging you from within, prodding you now to uproot your same-old-same-old and begin to construct a new personal and career identity?

Where is the fire in your belly coming from?

Knowing this will give you focus, clarity, and power behind your action steps. It energizes your search and fuels your determination to get where you want to go. Finding the fire in your belly can be one of the most defining moments in your life and career. Frankly, those who have found the fire in their belly usually work harder and smarter than those who don't.

Be warned: finding the fire in your belly takes time and can be an emotional roller coaster ride. But it will free power and awareness to stoke your mission toward your own success and happiness.

Now, ask yourself these questions, writing down the answers in the same notebook or place on your computer. It's even better to have someone else ask you the questions and allow yourself to free associate with your answers.

- Why do you want to change your career?
- What's motivating you to succeed?
- Why is it important to you now?
- What's the worst thing that would happen if you don't do this now?
- Imagine yourself 20 years from now. How will you feel if you don't make the career changes you want to make and are capable of now?
- Imagine yourself in your 60s. What does your life look like? Are you still working in a job you love? What do you want to feel proudest of as you look back in your career?

Keep asking yourself these questions until you experience a shift, an "ah-ha," or an emotional release. When you think you've answered the question, ask yourself, or have your friend question "why" until you know you have arrived at your right answer. When you've found the fire in your belly, you'll know it! Some refer to it as the "why until you cry."

In Chapter 2, we'll help you get in the best frame of mind for the work ahead. We'll show you how to avoid the traps of the victim mentality and the Facebook fallacy. We'll give you a few exercises to help you evaluate and boost your confidence, do a reality check about your successes and failures, and give you some attitude helpers as you move forward to find that great job.

NOTES

_____

_____

_____

_____

_____

_____

_____

_____

_____

_____

_____

_____

_____
_____
_____
_____
_____
_____
_____
_____
_____
_____
_____
_____
_____
_____
_____
_____
_____
_____
_____
_____
_____
_____
_____
_____
_____

_____

_____

_____

_____

_____

_____

_____

_____

_____

_____

_____

_____

_____

_____

_____

_____

_____

_____

_____

_____

_____

_____

_____

_____

_____

_____

_____

_____

_____

_____

_____

_____

_____

_____

_____

_____

_____

_____

_____

_____

_____

_____

_____

_____

_____

_____

_____

_____

CHAPTER 2:

Failures are
Perfectly Fine!

Finding your "why" can be fun, but it's not a Fast-Pass to the front of the career line. How often have you seen a friend apply for the dream job of a lifetime, and land it seamlessly? Not many, we're guessing. The fact is, failures happen, and it's actually an essential ingredient for success, as we'll discuss later.

First, though, let's look at fear, which can come from many sources. Here's one we can tamp down immediately: the Facebook Fallacy. We live in a social-media-obsessed, anxiety-ridden culture, and when you go online to see other people out there achieving things, getting promotions, and having fun, you can feel like the last kid picked for the kickball team. The fallacy is that they are happy, self-assured, clear of their direction, and better than you. This is very likely not reality.

Underneath those big smiles, just about everyone has similar fears that things are going to start crumbling around them. Everyone! No matter how polished someone's persona seems, no matter how strong their voice or how wide their smiles, everyone fakes it to some degree. No one is 100% confident all the time.

But confidence will be key to your success in networking, just like Angie's story in Chapter 1. Confidence helps overcome obstacles, and push past rejection and self-doubt. So consider how you have already proven yourself. Recall past successes. How hard did you work? How much did you stretch yourself and put yourself out there? How did you feel when you came out on top? That's where we want you to be right now.

But we also understand how strong those confidence-killers can be. So let's take a closer look.

The Victim Mentality

When we face hardships and life challenges, we sometimes succumb to the victim mentality, which will slowly drain the confidence out of anyone. When you feel that life is happening to you (rather than for you), and when you subconsciously make a habit of feeling sorry for yourself, the victim mentality is maintaining its grip. If you're not where you think you should be, or doing what you want to be doing, you may have made an unfortunately comfy bed for yourself in the role of the perpetual victim.

Not sure if that's you? Take a moment and ask yourself the following questions:

- Do you complain a lot?
- Do you look at other people's successes and feel bitter, envious, and jealous?
- Do you feel like you don't have any control over anything that happens in your life?

It's natural to think, "Oh, that must be nice," when you look at images of your colleagues on vacation in Sun Valley or at their summer home on Martha's Vineyard. But if your anger, jealousy, or bitterness is intense and your thoughts automatically complain, "I could never have that" or, "that should be me instead, but I got screwed"—you're stuck inside a victim mentality. It's not easy to move past this kind of thought process, but it's essential to move in a forward direction and become proactive instead of reactive.

A change of perspective is in order. And yeah, it's tough to all of a sudden admire and celebrate people you've resented. So start small. When you're driving and somebody cuts you off, resist the urge to honk the horn, scream profanities, or speed up to cut them off. Instead, take a breath and consider why they cut you off. Maybe they were late for a critical doctor's appointment for their sick child, or maybe they were going to lose their job if they were late again. Maybe they were just jerks, but you get the point: turn your anger into curiosity. Eventually, this will help you shift your mindset on friends and colleagues to thinking the best of them instead of the worst.

When you see others being successful, take a moment and ask yourself what steps they were willing to take to get where they are. Are those steps you would be willing to take as well? If not, why are you comparing? What are some steps you can take to move in the direction you want to go? Instead of being intimidated by others, let yourself be inspired by them. Let that inspiration help you clarify your vision for yourself and fuel your efforts to achieve it. It's your choice. If nothing else, at least be able to say, "If they can accomplish that, there's no question I can accomplish at least that!"

This extends to work, as well. If a leader or manager rejects your idea or makes you feel less than worthy in any way, the natural, reactive inclination is to blow off steam with a coworker, stew at your desk, or indulge in an extra round at happy hour. Don't. Tap into your new proactive skills instead. Write down the idea for another time, and take a close look at your points: was there a key piece of research or information missing? Maybe your idea would be better suited to another department, time or another company altogether. Remain curious.

It's time to work at becoming successful. Let's say you've had a string of failures recently. That's okay. Start to look at them from a new perspective and turn those failures into wins. How? By extracting the lessons learned from each and every experience. Within each failure, there were inevitably some things that you learned and can apply to your career, the steps you take to make decisions, and your efforts pushing forward. Even if something ended badly, ask yourself what you can learn from the experience? How can you grow from it? What can you do better, differently, or more successfully next time? Once you have discovered these things, and start to act on them, then you turn your failure into a win. We like to call this failing forward toward success.

Dream Big—With Work, Time, and Courage

Have you ever seen lions chase gazelles? The lions often fail to overcome their prey, but they keep going. Now, the lion could think: "Oh darn, I missed another gazelle. So why should I even bother trying again? I'm going to go eat some snails instead." But that's not what a lion thinks. Instead, the lion is always thinking of opportunity. "Okay, I missed that one. But hey, there are twelve more gazelles out there. I'll get the next one!"

Because it sees the opportunities, it knows what it's inherently built to do, so it keeps trying. The game's not over until either you win, or you say it's over. You have to keep pushing forward. Maybe you're already a lion—you're confident and opportunistic, but you've failed and feel frustrated. You haven't found the formula yet. Either way, over time, you will succeed. (And please note: we actually have no idea what a lion thinks.)

Like you, we've heard all the phrases in the book when it comes to applying yourself. It doesn't come easy. You get what you put into it. Success requires work, time, courage, and a great deal of determination. You have to be persistent, tenacious, and unwavering. You have to learn about yourself, test yourself, push yourself, and stretch out of your comfort zone.

But this advice sticks around for a reason: it works. Maybe you *have* failed. But the more of yourself, your time, and your effort you dedicate toward a goal, the more options and opportunities will present themselves along your journey. Investing in yourself is the *only* way to make a change. So it's time for another check-in on your goals.

- Who do you want to be?
- What are you willing to do for that?
- Are you up for the challenge?

While you're at it, dream big. You have to dream big to achieve big—whatever that means for you. If it means finding a job that you enjoy and hold onto for 50 years—great. If it means climbing the corporate ladder or someday owning your own business—fantastic. But don't short-change yourself by setting goals that are too easy.

People with deep-seated confidence give themselves permission to think and dream big and take the right steps to achieve big. If you're not solutions-driven and thinking about the bigger picture and where you want to be 10, 20, or 30 years down the road, you will end up selling yourself short. If you think to yourself, "I'm just a project manager," "just a truck driver," "just an office manager" or "just an accountant," you're missing your bigger picture and you're doing yourself a disservice. We all have the opportunity to be something more.

If you want more for yourself, then go out and grab it. What do you have to lose? Returning to our discussion in Chapter 1, what's your worst-case scenario? With consistent investment of time and effort, you'll be financially and personally more successful than you would have thought possible. You might actually discover you're genuinely happy.

That's the ultimate goal, right? Why not go for it? Give yourself permission to set that Big Hairy Audacious Goal (B-HAG) and let that enrich your confidence. Then set a few smaller achievable goals in support of your B-HAG—and knock them out of the park.

Success Builds Over Time

Nelson Mandela once famously said. "I never lose. Either I win or learn." And he was right. Each so-called loss or failure is actually a great learning opportunity. Interestingly, many industry leaders we've talked with tell us they find as much value in what people have learned from their failures as they do from their successes. When viewed through a different lens, most failures have the potential to be turned around and turned into personal successes.

Let's say you lost a tennis match, 6–0. As an achievement-oriented person, you'd go out and get a lesson or two, right? Or you failed to deliver some critical paperwork to a client before the deadline. It sounds like a good time to work on your project management skills, including automatic alerts to remind you of a key milestone ahead. And you don't have to pay a dime or any of this, as it's all online, from a virtual tennis coach to such tools as Trello, Asana, and beyond.

Don't even know where to begin? Ask for help. A friend of ours who works in a shared office space was struggling to create a new Trello project management board when a guy came into the common area to microwave his daily ramen. She asked if he knew

Trello—and it turns out the guy had actually *worked* at Trello for many years. Bingo.

Know Where You Shine—And Where You Don't

You can't get to where you want to go unless you first know where you are. Be honest with yourself about your strengths and weaknesses.

Drew's Story

Josh recently worked with a client named Drew, who'd wanted to be an attorney since high school. He passed the bar, landed a lucrative job as a lawyer—and discovered he had no passion for it; there was no shine in his career. But he *did* have a passion for learning how to hack—how to simplify and improve a wide variety of tasks, especially through technology. So he learned how to write code and found a job as a programmer paying significantly less money. Seven years later, he's more than tripled his salary and is managing teams in his growing career and company. But more importantly, he'd discovered where he didn't shine, and where he did.

One of the best ways to discover your own strengths and weaknesses is to ask others. Encourage them to be honest, and write down their answers. Absorb and analyze their insights. Do you agree with them? Why or why not? Personality and ability tests such as DISC, Enneagram, and Gallup Strengths-Finder are also valuable and affordable investments.

Once you discover, understand, and own your strengths and weaknesses, you'll be better equipped to talk about them honestly, effectively, and confidently in any context— but especially in an interview. Let's say a personality test has revealed you're pretty much a linear thinker. You think: First 1. Then 2. Then 3.

Some people might see this as a weakness or an inability to "go with the flow" and be flexible in your thought process. But if you know this about yourself, and if you understand how it has been both beneficial in some situations and a hindrance in others, you can focus the conversation on the value of this strength. You can share how you are able to bring order to chaos and work with creative teams to bring their ideas through to creation. You will be more conscious about when you should "go with the flow" and when you can add value by implementing a process to achieve goals. And you will be able to share this value with your interviewer.

That's just one example of how a deep examination of your strengths and weaknesses can pay off big time in your career path. Being vulnerable and honest with yourself about your performance and experiences will uncover more of your strengths, build your confidence, and help you see yourself as a valuable asset to prospective businesses.

Exercise: Successes and Failures

Take your list of successes and accomplishments that you started in Chapter 1 and reflect on each experience. Write down as much detail about those events as possible. Create as many metrics—measurements that compare the before and after pictures of your accomplishments—as you can. They might be related to finances, time, process, accomplishments, learning, speed, quantity, quality, or other things. For example, you might say, "I was able to increase our sales revenue by 5% by offering an additional incentive," or "I increased our pipeline by 30% by implementing a specific communications process," or "By using routing software, I was able to save our technicians 1.5 hours a day in reduced drive time and reduce fuel and maintenance costs 15%."

Having such a list like this at your fingertips will be helpful for you when you're interviewing. You'll be able to reference your successes, know how they are relevant, and express how they will help the manager and the company solve relevant problems and meet their goals. You'll be able to share the stories speaking to their needs without having to think about them. These few steps will even help you ask great questions—questions that relate to what your prospective employer considers important and make you look interested and capable. They will demonstrate that you can clearly identify pain points, challenges, and obstacles and successfully navigate through or around them. And that will help set you apart from the competition. But for now, the process will give you insight into where you shine and help you build your confidence.

Next, write down all your failures. Once again, be honest with yourself. It's not only *okay* if the list of your failures is a little longer than your successes—it's also *completely* normal. Write out all the gory details of each of your failures and things you've had a part in that failed. They might range from "I broke the company coffee pot" to "I got fired after recklessly driving my 4Runner right through the office's front doors." Take each one individually and ask:

- Why did I/we fail?
- What have I learned from the experience?
- How can I apply what I've learned to ensure future success?

Acknowledge your part and responsibility in the failure. If you're focusing on what others did wrong ("Mike left the coffee pot on the counter," or "My spouse made me lose control of the car by texting me"), you're missing the point. The process will help you identify your weaknesses, wounds, and battle scars. It's common to find areas where you unintentionally sabotaged your own success, or where a fear prevented you from doing something challenging or seeing an opportunity. You'll develop the power not to do them again and to practice better patterns of behavior, if only through trial and error. It will help you do things differently when faced with similar situations, challenges, or conflicts. We can't encourage you enough to be completely vulnerable and honest with yourself. These insights will be invaluable to you.

Once you've completed your honest assessment of your failures and any embarrassing experiences in your life, it's time for more reflection. Ask yourself the following questions, writing down the answers:

- What would I have done differently knowing what I know now?
- Where have I applied things I've learned from each of these failures?
- Did these failures have a positive impact on me or my colleagues in later endeavors? How?
- How and why does this better position me and the company where I work for future success?

Now, you'll exude confidence and value when you can say something like: "I appreciate all I learned at Company X. While it wasn't a huge success, what I learned while I was there made a very positive impact on me personally and professionally. Here's how..." Being able to talk about how you've handled and grown from your learning experiences will set you apart. You will appear more capable, genuine, and attractive compared to those who have not invested the time to reflect on these things, learn from them, and apply them to their professional and personal lives.

In fact, you'll actually come across in a very favorable light. You might find that, instead of backing away, people will begin to lean into your story. They might recognize something in it that they can relate to, something that resonates with them and thus builds rapport between you.

Adam's Story ———————————

Adam was a division head of R&D for a very large mobile device provider when he told Josh about his failure. He thought it was going to be an amazing opportunity, but soon learned that the company didn't want to implement his—or anyone else's—new and fresh ideas. They wanted to keep their cash cows rolling along. And they really missed the ball. Their competitors capitalized on it and ultimately out-innovated them—and hit a home run. Adam's company had once been a household name but is now little more than a footnote. While this was a painful and costly decision and experience for him, he now recognizes that he should have invested more time up-front learning about the company direction, leadership, and commitment to innovation rather than being excited about a brand name. Adam learned from that experience and now makes better decisions. He doesn't have to be negative toward the company, and he knows there's no value in bashing anybody he worked with or for. He learned an important lesson and walked away with a little bit of a battle scar. Today, his career is flourishing.

One more note here: Sometimes it's a really fruitful exercise to discuss with your previous employer why things went south. If you are able to reach a former employer and discuss your performance, circumstances, and situation at the time, you'll get clear feedback about your strengths and weaknesses. While it might be sobering at first, it can be profoundly empowering.

Attitude Helpers

We've found that these perspectives can help build your confidence and energize your path to success:

Define what "success" means to you. If you don't define it, it's hard to know when you have succeeded. You will also end up seeing others' accomplishments as "success" without really knowing how it applies to your life and the story you want it to tell.

Take note of how others achieved success. When you see someone who's successful, take a moment to take note of what they did to achieve that success. Then try to apply what you learn by observing their success to improve your own results. Success is duplicatable.

Surround yourself with successful, resourceful, supportive people. They'll have a major impact on your attitude, your focus, and your ability to be successful in the things you want, both personally and professionally. If you surround yourself with people who are more invested in the latest reality show than in their own lives, chances are you will invest less in your own life as well.

Discover who wants you in their circle. What does this tell you about you, the direction you are headed, and your probability of being successful, both professionally and personally?

Use your Why as rocket fuel. Change "I'll never amount to anything so I won't even bother trying" to "I'm never going to allow those people to be right!" Use that energy to push yourself until you reach your desired success.

Remember, you haven't written your whole story yet. So don't let yourself go negative or allow doubt to keep you from trying your hardest.

Take charge of your career. It's okay to want something and shoot for it. It's okay to ask others for help in getting there. It's okay to ask a boss and peers to help you chart a path to success. It's even okay to shoot for something uncommon. Just remember, you might have to do uncommon things to get there. You're writing your own story here. What actions do you want to take to get you where you want to be?

Fake it till you make it. Okay, truth be told, there simply will be times when you just have to appear confident even when you aren't feeling it. When ignorance is mutual, confidence is king.

Do not be cocky. Apply what you learn to the decisions you make with humility.

Ask good questions and listen actively. Listening can not only help you appear more confident and capable than you feel you are at the time, but it will also help you make better decisions and help those around you feel more confident and comfortable with the decisions being made. Even if you're not the one making the decisions, asking the questions that help lead to a better decision or solution makes you the most valuable person in the room.

Run your own race. Don't be distracted by how anyone else is doing or what they're saying. Focus on doing and being the best you can be. Make the best decisions you can make; truly give 100% of your efforts. Push yourself to do something uncommon every day to push yourself forward. End each day knowing you've done your best.

Now that you've gotten a good grip on your successes and failures, it's time to take them out in the world and use them to promote your product—yourself.

NOTES

_____

_____

_____

_____

_____

_____

_____

_____

_____

_____

_____

_____

_____

_____

_____

_____

_____

_____

_____

_____

_____

_____

_____

_____

_____

_____

_____

_____

_____

_____

_____

_____

_____

_____

_____

_____

_____

_____

_____

_____

_____

_____

_____

_____

_____

_____

_____

_____

_____

_____

_____

_____

_____

_____

_____

_____

_____

_____

_____

_____

_____

_____

_____

_____

_____

_____

_____

_____

_____

_____

_____

_____

_____

_____

CHAPTER 3:

Who Are You, Anyway?

What if you could put yourself on a shelf? All boxed up, just waiting to catch the eye of the next customer shopping for a new employee. Inside yourself, you have plenty of accomplishments, successes and failures that make you valuable to them. You're almost bursting at the seams with your history, skills, and desire for a more satisfying career. But your packaging...well, that might need some work. The customer notices the next box, with precise, plastic-wrapped corners and all jazzed up with colors and promises.

Viewing yourself as a "product" might change the way you think about yourself in the work world. You are now a product in a marketplace. It's time to start viewing your job search as an exercise in marketing and "selling" the product (you) to the best possible customers (employers).

You can also imagine yourself as a character in a book. How would the author describe you, your strengths, weaknesses, and your skills?

Either way, stepping outside of yourself for a moment allows you to see how customers—in this case, prospective employers—see you. So you waste less time emotionally judging yourself as a person. This allows you to focus on what the market wants and needs instead of what *you* need. And with that clarity, you're in a better position to learn precisely what attributes, experiences and attitudes your prospective employers are actually seeking in a candidate (product)—even if they're not completely clear about it themselves.

Only you can get your product right for the marketplace. If that product is missing parts, prospective employers and your networks will fill in the gaps with their own ideas of who you are. They'll make assumptions when thinking about what you have to offer and whether it's valuable. If you don't define yourself, you will be dependent on assumptions and descriptions other people place on you. It's not a promising scenario.

Branding Yourself

By taking the time to define for yourself who you are as a product, you can come up with a clear and consistent message so companies can quickly see why they should hire you. You have a "brand" in the minds of your potential employers and people in your network—and it will be at the forefront of a strong and convincing online presence that works for you 24/7. The No. 1 piece of advice we can give here is to keep consistent. If you put yourself on the "physical therapist" shelf and then jump to the "virtual assistant" shelf a month later, it creates a confusing message. Make it easy for prospective employers to find you, read about you, discover some delightful surprises, and ultimately decide to hire you.

Everyday Value

Once you are willing to see yourself as a product for hire in a marketplace, you can start asking and answering critical questions in your quest for a new position, such as:

- How do I add value to organizations?

- What skills do I have that are most valuable?
- What's the best way to communicate my value?
- Who needs my skills and abilities?
- When am I most valuable?
- Why would someone hire me?
- Where in an organization's life cycle am I most valuable?

When you define yourself as a product and identify your value, you make it much easier for a company to see you as a solution to their pain points, as a problem-solver, and as someone who will lean their shoulder in to contribute to the success of the company. You'll be able to spell out exactly why you're what the company is looking for. Imagine yourself saying:

- "I'm able to add value to your team by_____."
- "I can help you accomplish your goal because of my experience with_____."
- "I can help you overcome your obstacles so that you can achieve your mission as I've done with _____."
- Or "I can help unify your team by creating _____."

Good hiring managers love it when you help them connect the dots like this because you're literally speaking their language.

Do what you love? Or what you're good at?

Many books today, it seems, implore you to find a job doing what you love and what you have a passion for, which is all well and good. But thinking only what you want, think, feel, or need can prevent a realistic career transition strategy. We like to point out that there's a difference between what you want to do or love to do, and what you can do that adds real value to others. Josh, for example, would love to wakeboard, surf, fish, and ride four-wheelers up in the mountains every day, but unfortunately, he hasn't yet figured out how to turn those activities into significant revenue streams.

Ignoring the ways we can benefit others can blind us to opportunities where we can experience the most success, accomplishment, and, ultimately, joy. Take a minute to consider your failures. When you look back at them from a higher perspective, you might decide that, ultimately, they fall in the win column of the broader view of your life. Work can follow the same path sometimes. A sense of fulfillment only really comes after you put in the hard work. If we felt at the top of our game every minute of every day, then we wouldn't be able to differentiate or appreciate our wins.

In the long run, many find that the things they are proudest of and the areas where they excelled were not necessarily the things they enjoyed the most. From our experience, we've found that work is what you do so you have results you can enjoy and be most proud of. Additionally, others will appreciate and value you more when they know you have worked hard to accomplish something.

While most jobs come with their own particular office politics and some challenges, as you progress through your career journey, you'll find that there are workplaces that offer company cultures aligning with who you are. In Chapter 6, we will describe how you can find the workplaces that better complement who you are and the benefits that align with your value.

Calculating Your Worth

The following exercises will help you hone your concepts of the value you offer as well as help you discover how prospective employers might view you as an attractive product. As you go through the exercises, feel free to reference the accomplishments, successes, and failures you identified in Chapters 1 and 2.

Exercise: Your Value

Ask yourself these questions, writing down the answers.

- What do I do that's valuable to others?
- Why is it valuable?
- Where and when is it valuable?
- To whom is it valuable?
- How can I add value to organizations and teams?
- How do I communicate my value efficiently and make it memorable?

Exercise: Your Product Message

Hone your product message by connecting the dots between what you do, what you offer to others, and what outcome they are seeking. To do so, fill in the following sentence for each one of your relevant, valuable skills:

I help _[who]_ be, do, or have _[proposed outcome]_ so that _[their desired result]._

These exercises can be emotionally tough and frustrating. Be present with your emotions but don't allow your frustrations to win. The process can be incredibly helpful and offer you insights into where and how you can thrive and be most successful. Frustration and anger can lead to amazing revelations that cut to the core of your true value. All of this will help you communicate why you are a great hire in a way that most cannot.

This sentence-building exercise can be the cornerstone of your messaging. Use it frequently and revise it as you learn more about how others see your value to them. As you grow, so will your messaging.

Exercise: What Environments Bring Out the Best in You?

Write down your answers to these questions:

- What are you really good at?
- What roles did you excel in?
- What results from your efforts are you proudest of?
- What have you enjoyed about these roles? Why?
- What roles didn't you enjoy? Why?

- What do you feel your abilities and skills give you the ability to accomplish in future roles?
- What challenges would be exciting for you to take on?
- What do these answers tell you about the types of companies and positions that you will thrive in?

Your answers will help you identify and understand where you're more likely to excel—where you typically add the most value. Later, you'll also use your answers to build qualifying questions for interviewing, networking, and landing just the right job.

Finding a Peer Group

Now you can take things to the next level by getting some help from your friends and colleagues (we'll discuss this more in Chapter 5). Pick five to seven people you respect—even choose a few beyond your peer group—and ask for their help with your project of clarifying your value to the working world.

Do: Be selective. See if you can enlist people who you are just a little afraid to ask for help. Find people who will be straight with you when you do or say something crazy or when you're unknowingly fooling yourself or being myopic. Make an effort to seek out people who look at things with a critical eye and are willing to ask better and tougher questions. Once they say "Yes," give them full permission to be unfiltered, raw, and completely straight with you.

Don't: Reach out to people you know are simply going to be accommodating and agreeable. You're not looking for cheerleaders here.

Do: Be aware that some of your potential supporters are actually in a similar spot as you, and you can help them in return. They might be in the same boat—looking for a job, thinking about a career change, interested in rebranding themselves—and wanting to collaborate with you as you both hold each other accountable and push each other toward successes.

Don't: Take this process lightly. It will give you a significant advantage in growing your career. You'll get honest feedback from others. You will be able to see and help others who are struggling with something you've already overcome. It also makes you a great collaborator who will attract a higher caliber of people, which, of course, raises your game. It will also help you build your network, your credibility, and your ability to leverage your network.

Exercise: Get Input from Friends and Colleagues

Ask the members of your new peer group to ask you the questions below. If they're in the same boat as you, return the favor and ask them the questions, too! While we posed some of these questions in previous chapters, reviewing them again may, in fact, elicit new memories and perspectives that can be helpful to your process.

- Where have you been successful?
- What are your biggest accomplishments?
- What are some of your proudest moments?
- What makes you valuable?
- What are your biggest failures?
- What did you learn from them?
- Where has what you've learned from your failures helped you succeed at something?
- Where do you want to take your career? Why?
- What are the next logical steps for you to take in your career? Why?
- What do coworkers and leaders typically want you to be involved in? Why?

Chances are your supporters will ask follow-up questions simply out of curiosity—further enhancing your self-awareness and value.

Mentors and significant others

In addition to your team of peer supporters, connect with two or three mentors who you can absolutely trust to give you honest feedback. Be prepared for the fact it can be difficult to ask for help from some of these people, such as the in-laws who have always frowned upon you. They'll probably be happy to help you be more successful and give you constructive feedback.

Tony's Story

Recently, Josh worked with a client named Tony, who was about a year out of college, working in sales in Atlanta. He decided that he wanted to do better financially and be V.P. of Sales of a software company one day. He wasn't the worst performer, and definitely not the best performer, but a good, solid, middle-of-the-pack guy.

So Tony ended up jumping on LinkedIn, finding a dozen VP of sales at technology companies. When he reached out for advice on taking the right steps, Josh encouraged him to ask some of the VPs about mentoring. Sure enough, a few of them were open to it, and Tony took each of them out to lunch to create a mentoring plan. Pretty soon, they had a regular schedule going. Josh was impressed by not only Tony's fortitude in presenting himself as a well-packaged product, but also the consistency of their meetings. He's now director of sales for a growing company on the West Coast, and his mentors brag about Tony being their mentee. Them working together created the type of valuable relationships that helped Tony build an impactful and intentional career.

People Who Can Help Test Your Value

Once you've got a good sense of your value, it's time to test the waters beyond your comfort zone. Here are some contacts who will help you get an even more precise measurement of what you're worth.

Your former boss, boss's boss, or another leader whose comments intimidated you. Be fearless and shameless with this. Find people who will make things wonderfully and impactfully more difficult for you; by helping you grow, they'll actually make things easier for you in the long game. The worst they can say is, "no."

A new acquaintance at a dinner party or networking event (a guinea pig). You've just been introduced to someone for the first time. Even though they aren't traditionally in your support group, don't discount them. Maneuver in one of your working value statements. It may feel awkward, but it is valuable market research for re-defining yourself and what you do. Listen to how others react to your product messaging as you share it and how they choose to describe you if they are introducing you after you've shared it.. As they begin to introduce you to their network, you'll start hearing what people think you do, which can be an amazing eye-opener. You might even get further inspired by how someone shares your messaging or experience. (For example: "Meet Trisha. She's gotta be the world's top expert on how entrepreneurship impacts marriages.) This is a great indicator of how successful you've been at defining yourself thus far, and where you still need help.

Your spouse, boyfriend, or girlfriend. This person is more capable of looking at you objectively because you've shared life and experiences, but in a different way. Fair warning: this can create some tension when they give you tough love along with encouragement. If you feel yourself getting resentful, angry, or frustrated with them, remember that they are likely the most valuable person in this process and in your life. Your significant other is one of the people who know you well enough to give you honest answers and who's also invested in the outcome. The clarity and quality of information will be worth the bumps and bruises to your ego. Hopefully, they will know when to be supportive and when to kick you in the butt—there's immense value in both.

Noticing Themes

As you spend time identifying your value, crafting your product value statements, and getting feedback from others, you'll notice how certain themes crop up. People may repeatedly tell you how much they respect the way you interact with others, or how well you problem-solve. You may have thought your obvious strength was building spreadsheets and analyzing numbers when, actually, the repetitive sentiment about you was your ability to corral and motivate them to take action. They're additional building blocks for defining yourself as a product and will help you quickly and succinctly communicate your value, no matter where you are.

Specifically, watch for areas where people value you or perceive you as an expert. Think about when people come and ask for your help, opinion, or advice. Are there areas where people seem to value you most or even seek your leadership or wisdom?

Josh's Story

As a recruiter, Josh started to notice themes in the ways he interacted with people. He'd get to know them on a deeper level and help them connect with other individuals in a mutually beneficial way. He discovered he was more than just a typical recruiter because of the way he listened to people. Over time, he began to recognize the themes in what people shared about how he added the most value. Josh heard from people how he was:

- identifying relevant talent and getting new hires on board in a timely way;
- maximizing recruiting spend (reducing their cost per hire);
- streamlining the recruiting process to eliminate the hassles around communication and poor workflow.

These issues came up for his clients repeatedly—and he realized he was really good at solving them.

When he took the time to identify those three themes, he very quickly sharpened his messaging about his own value. He tried variations of his new messaging on about 20 or 30 people and settled on one simple statement: "I help clients reduce the time, costs and hassles of hiring and keeping great people."

Later, Josh realized that when people talked to him about their career decisions, they often needed advice and assistance with making good decisions. So he had a second market in addition to recruiting clients: candidates. Once he noticed that, he added to his message that he helps people in technology make great career decisions. Both of these messages are simple to remember, and as a result, friends and colleagues use them to introduce Josh. Now, his messaging is really working for him.

Evolving your sense of value and identifying yourself as a product calls for ongoing refinement. Once the words you say—and what others say about you—are impactful, memorable, and unique to you, the refinement process can slow down. Even then, you might evolve further, so plan to revisit all of this as you continue to grow professionally and personally.

Now that you can see the value of presenting yourself as a product in the job marketplace, it's time to learn how to respond to the needs of your customers and let them know you're here to help. Chapter 4 offers insight into identifying the pain points of your customers and the tools you can use to communicate that you care.

NOTES

_____
_____
_____
_____
_____
_____
_____
_____
_____
_____
_____
_____
_____
_____
_____
_____
_____
_____
_____

_____

_____

_____

_____

_____

_____

_____

_____

_____

_____

_____

_____

_____

_____

_____

_____

_____

_____

_____

_____

_____

_____

_____

_____

_____

_____

_____

_____

_____

_____

_____

_____

_____

_____

_____

_____

_____

_____

_____

_____

_____

_____

CHAPTER 4:

Communicating More Effectively

We care about you—we really do. It's why we're writing this for you. But we'll be brutally honest and say nobody else really gives a crap about what you think, feel, need, and want.

Dale Carnegie, author of the legendary *How to Win Friends and Influence People,* explains this reality. "Why talk about what we want?" he writes. "That is childish. Absurd. Of course, you are interested in what you want. You are eternally interested in it. But no one else is. The rest of us are just like you: we are interested in what we want. So the only way on earth to influence other people is to talk about what they want and show them how to get it."

The fact is, everybody else is wrapped up in everything going on in their own world—and these days, that's a lot. So it takes a different kind of communication to really tap into your network and break through barriers for your career.

Shifting the Focus

Open your phone right now and scroll to a random person. Now, ask yourself how much you really care about that person's career. Not so much, right? They probably have the exact same level of concern and care for your career.

Knowing this can work to your advantage. You can communicate more effectively, discover what they want, and make an impression on them that may ultimately get you a connection or a job. When you are better able to understand the thoughts, feelings, and needs of someone else, you are better able to convey the value you could add to their career and life. How you are a solution to their problems, and how you can help them achieve their goals is incredibly meaningful. Once you do that effectively...job offers.

"If there is any one secret of success, it lies in the ability to get the other person's point of view and see things from that person's angle as well as from your own." — **Henry Ford**

When you see things from other peoples' point of view, a whole world of opportunity opens up. You begin to see exactly how you can add value to them, and what introductions you can make from your side. Remember to show you are genuinely interested in *them* and their careers.

Business leaders are hungry for solutions-oriented people. When they find capable people with a "How can I help?" attitude, who seem to know the who/what/where/when/why/how of something, they value them highly. When you show them how and help them to get what they want, they'll remember you in a much more favorable way than someone simply seeking a new job. They'll also be more inclined to proactively help you when opportunities arise.

Asking the Right Questions

Listen to yourself talk for a moment. If you begin a lot of conversations with, "I want," "I feel," "I need," and "I think," then it's time for some communication inventory, which is actually pretty easy.

Just come up with questions you can ask people when there's a gap in the conversation. Replace "I"-centric statements with substantive questions like these:

- What challenges are you having with _____?
- What goals are you trying to accomplish at work or in _____?
- How can I help you with _____?
- What are some of the things that are going on in your organization around _____?
- What are some things you guys are trying to accomplish around _____?
- Would it be helpful to you to talk with someone in my network who's been through the same thing?

Now begin to imagine their responses. If you were to say, "I think you'll be impressed by my accomplishments," chances are they'll start thinking about what to order from UberEats. But when you ask an "other-centric" question, delving into something specific about their needs, wants, or goals, chances are they'll snap to attention. Even if they don't have specific answers, this is a much more effective way to communicate.

Let's say you're a web developer and you've seen Company Y's website crashing. You've connected with Company Y's manager through your network. Instead of immediately offering your services, ask the manager her needs. What might be causing the crashes? Offer potential solutions. If it turns out the problem is beyond your professional scope and you can't help them yourself, you still might be able to refer them to someone else who can help or otherwise point them in a useful direction.

Gaining Referrals

Once you've genuinely offered to help someone out of a bind, they will likely be more inclined to think about how they can help you in return. Maybe Company Y's manager will be ready for a website overhaul in 3 months or know someone else who is looking to establish a new web presence. Perhaps one of her colleagues is in the process of launching a new company that will require a website. Referrals come from people who appreciate your interest in them, followed up by your own background and skills.

One of Josh's clients was in a panic because he had a burst pipe and his basement was flooding. Josh walked him through the process of how to shut off his water, then showed up at his house 45 minutes later with the remediation gear to get the water out of the basement. They spent about an hour and a half sucking up water and moving stuff around to prevent further damage. The client ended up telling the story to a bunch of other people he knew and Josh ended up with new business relationships because he had spent a couple of hours at his client's house sucking water out of the basement and helping to minimize the damage.

"Warm" referrals—when the referring person stakes their own credibility to recommend you—are the best kind you can get. Your acts of kindness, work ethic, attitude, and good reputation have put you in an enviable position. Because of the introduction from someone they respect, leaders and companies will view you more as a trusted expert and peer instead of somebody just looking for a job. Word will spread that you are the go-to person within your professional community and more opportunities will come knocking at your door.

Creating a Lasting Impression

Pay attention to personal details with your connections. They might mention an anniversary dinner or a child's name; make a mental note during the conversation or something else personal and unique. Keep track of the details in a journal or online tool. Reference them in conversation; call them on their birthday or anniversary. When you can mention something personal that you previously discussed with them, it shows people you pay attention and are genuinely interested in them.

> You'd be surprised to learn how many people Josh calls to wish happy birthday and then have them turn around and say, "Wow. Thanks, Josh. You're actually the only person who called me today." It's so easy to post a "Happy Birthday" on Facebook or other social media sites. Calling someone to personally say "Happy Birthday" really isn't any more difficult and shows that you care about them enough to actually call.

Crabs in the Bucket

Start noticing where others are on the give-versus-take scale. Who are the givers and who are all about take-take-take? You'll see how people don't just take, they also make things worse by bringing a destructive air to conversations—bad-mouthing others, complaining or gossiping frequently, or always expressing a victim mentality where nothing is ever their fault or responsibility. We call this kind of people "crabs in the bucket." While so many of us are working hard to build our careers and lives doing the right things, sometimes people will pull you down and use you for leverage to climb over you to get ahead themselves. Picture a bucket with a bunch of crabs in it. They all want to get out of the bucket but don't know how to work together or worse, aren't willing to work together to get out. We'd encourage you to not be tempted to jump in the bucket with people like this. It's a trap. These are the kind of people who don't do much of their own work to get ahead and they don't care who they hurt in the process. They aren't very attractive to those of us that are willing to help others and put in the time and effort to accomplish something more or get somewhere new. And if you're a crab in the bucket, acknowledge it to yourself and return to our earlier sections on negative talk and victim mentality. With new awareness comes the power to change and grow.

Move away from the crabs in the bucket and surround yourself with a strong group of substantive leaders, doers, and peers—the positive influencers. (We'll discuss this more in Chapter 5.)

Exercise: Becoming More Aware

Here's another great exercise to build your awareness about contributing to people and having a positive impact: Become a student of what people say with their body language, facial expressions, and eye contact in reaction to what you or others are sharing.

Start by noticing any subtle changes indicating thoughts or feelings.

Body language: Do they lean in toward the conversation, or withdraw from it? How about their posture? Are they standing up straight or are they slumped over? Are their arms crossed across their chest (putting up a barrier), down by their side, or somewhere in between?

Facial expressions: Do they look happy, pensive, sad, angry, or frightened? What precipitated the change? What are they reacting to?

Eye contact: Are they maintaining a steady gaze, or glancing at what's going on around you?

Check out the placement of their arms. When and to what was shared or what's the cause of this reaction? What does this say about them and their feelings?

Noticing how people react physically to conversations is one more step toward communicating effectively. It will also help you pay attention to your own cues. Lean in, stand up straight with shoulders back arms at your side; and maintain eye contact with genuine interest. You'll likely notice more engagement from those you are talking with.

NOTES

_____

_____

_____

_____

_____

_____

_____

_____

_____

_____

_____

_____

_____

_____

_____

_____

_____

_____

_____

_____

_____

_____

_____

_____

_____

_____

_____

_____

_____

_____

_____

_____

_____

_____

_____

_____

_____

_____

_____

_____

CHAPTER 5

Expanding Your Network: Positive Influencers

If Trish were inviting people to a party and included Oprah, Tim Ferriss, Brené Brown, Mark Cuban, and Dwayne "The Rock" Johnson, would they show up? Doubtful! They have no clue who Trish is. But these people do grace our lives with their positive influence: we watch their shows and TED talks; read their books; and follow their Instagram feeds.

Closer to home, our lists might include our favorite bosses, our parents, our fun friends, and our spiritual leaders. It's up to you to surround yourself with the people who are going to provide the best possible influence on you, your career, your network, and your credibility. If you lie down with dogs, as the saying goes, you'll wake up with fleas. Tell us who your friends are, meanwhile, and we'll tell you who you are.

We must embrace how much we affect together. The people we hang out with, work with, live with, and follow on social media all have an influence on our decisions and our future direction. Consider the people who are in your social and professional circles right now and answer these questions.

- What do you notice about the attitudes, behaviors, and personalities of the people you are surrounding yourself with?
- Do you want to be more like them?
- Do you want to have what they have or live like they do?
- Do you want to have more of the qualities that you admire in them?
- Or do they reflect more of the qualities that you don't like so much in yourself?
- Who are the ones who don't have a positive impact on you, others, and community?
- What do you think others think of you based on who you associate with? (Other people

"grade" us based on the company we keep, too.)

- Are you comfortable with your answers? What do you want to change up?

In professional circles, people often make the mistake of surrounding themselves only with fun, easy going people. But nobody in those circles pushes or challenges them beyond their personal status quo. The same is true in personal relationships, where comfort and predictability are key. But to grow professionally and personally, you can't just fill your personal and professional social circles with safe people.

Change your environment, change yourself. Once you surround yourself with people who are forward-moving, aggressive, and excited about trying to accomplish things and change or move the world, then you'll find yourself getting caught up in that energy and find yourself accomplishing more yourself.

If you want to launch yourself into a higher level of self-expression, productivity, and rewards, you have to be open to new and more interesting things and engage in more challenging activities and behaviors. To do so, surround yourself with people who will influence you to move in those directions. We call them positive influencers. They are surprisingly good at influencing, motivating, and inspiring people without even trying.

The Power of Positive Influencers

Positive influencers tend to have several characteristics in common:

Hard Work and Humility

- They get things done but often don't expect or ask for credit
- They take responsibility for a job and follow through until it's completed
- Their attitude is that the game isn't over 'til they succeed

---

Value-Added Knowledge

- Others value their thoughts and opinions
- They often have ideas or suggestions to share or from a book they're reading that is relevant and helpful to others
- They genuinely care about people

Leadership

- They look for and find solutions when everyone else is complaining
- They guide teams through tough situations
- They lift others up and help them accomplish things
- They have a positive impact on those around them

Accountability

- They aren't afraid to admit they made a mistake
- They're open to seeking wise counsel for advice and solutions
- They not only say what they will do, but also when they'll do it
- They follow up on things

We've found many job-hunters today are overly concerned with how large their network is. Instead, try curating a smaller inner circle for the maximum impact. The size of your network can be a helpful measure of your reach, and we'll discuss that more in the next chapter. But it's important to pay attention to quality, especially when you're working to forward your career journey.

Exercise: Who Do I Want to Be?

Positive influencers have yet another positive influence. As you explore who they are, you also discover more about who you are. It's another cool step in job hunting and career changes to define and refine yourself.

Make a list of the people you admire and appreciate: Again, it could be anyone from Mother Teresa and Puff Daddy to your own mom and dad.

Write down their best characteristics and traits. Use the guide above as a reference.

Ask yourself, "How much do I want to be a person who thinks and acts in those ways?"

Take action. This starts with a simple list with the very next steps to becoming more of the person you want to be. You might decide to:

- Tell others what you appreciate about them
- Set reading goals with books (like this one) that will challenge you and help you grow
- Invest in others without expectation of return
- Say thank you more often

- Expect less and give more
- Stand up for someone or something you believe in
- Listen more and talk less
- Be more proactive instead of reactive

By the time you've worked through this list, we'll bet, you'll already be carrying yourself with a bit more self-awareness, self-confidence, and self-accountability—ideal for building relationships with those admirable people. Good stuff.

Assembling an Advisory Board

The next layer of your network is your Trusted Advisory Board, or TAB, a group of up to ten peers, mentors, and leaders who will both encourage you and help keep you focused and accountable as you move forward on your career journey.

Your TAB is uniquely suited to helping you maximize and achieve your career goals by understanding your value and honing your message. To get started, find three to seven of your peers you respect (notice we didn't say "like") who will be brutally honest with you while also helping you push through challenges. Keep in mind you'll have to cast a wide net to find these people; it's not just the first three to seven you think of! Their job will be to ask you pointed questions, keep you accountable, and give you feedback on your brand and your messaging. They'll tell you what they see about the choices and progress you're making.

One of Josh's passions is wakeboarding. It took him more than 100 painful tries to land his first flip (heelside back roll). When he knew he was close to nailing it, the anticipation was intoxicating, and when he finally did it, he was ecstatic. But he actually felt more joy and excitement from mentoring a friend and being with him when he landed his first flip. It was so much more rewarding and thrilling than Josh's own personal accomplishment. When you ask someone to be a mentor, they also receive value and joy from the relationship.

We also recommend that your TAB include people of the same gender as you. As much as we champion diversity, we also find that sometimes men and women are not truly able to "be themselves" with the opposite gender because of discomfort, bravado, insecurity, not wanting to feel weak, or power dynamics. Our goal here is for you to surround yourself with a group of thoughtful and impactful people who will be able to challenge and guide you without pretense, without judgment, and without gender bias.

Every other week, meet with your TAB to make sure you're on the right path and that you're consistently working to define yourself as a product. The more you interact with them, the more they'll confidently and comfortably refer you to others looking for expertise in your wheelhouse. We've talked about the support, clarity, and energy you get from aligning yourself with a growing network and a team that will walk with you on your career journey. Next, you'll learn how to find the people, companies, and positions that will help you pinpoint your best-fitting job.

NOTES

_____

_____

_____

_____

_____

_____

_____

_____

_____

_____

_____

_____

_____

_____

_____

_____

_____

_____

_____

_____

_____

_____

_____

_____

_____

_____

_____

_____

_____

_____

_____

_____

_____

_____

_____
_____
_____
_____
_____
_____
_____
_____
_____
_____
_____
_____
_____
_____
_____
_____
_____
_____
_____
_____
_____
_____

CHAPTER 6:

Applying Yourself

Y ou've just learned several core principles that will speed you through the process of finding a job within a competitive marketplace. We have discussed how to re-evaluate the benefits of "running toward" what you want instead of "running from" what you don't want, even though the habit of running *from* stuff may have been running *you* for a long time. You've taken the time to review your career so far, revisit several of your success stories, and acknowledge any or all of your best accomplishments. You've even re-imagined your failures, and you appreciate more than ever the lessons those experiences have conferred upon you that will bring you future success.

Most importantly, you've begun to get a grasp of how you can define yourself as a product that potential employers, coworkers, and even your work community will consider to be needed, valuable, and even necessary. You're already miles ahead of the competition. You have the ingredients you need to find that well-fitting, rewarding job where you can shine and add your unique value to a company.

Yes, you have the ingredients, but you don't yet have the recipe. That's what this chapter is about: how to put it all together. This chapter gives you the insights and tricks of the trade to launch an effective, targeted, smart, and persistent game plan for finding great jobs with great companies. You'll find easy-to-follow methods for significantly better response rates to help you find an amazing job that brings out all the best that you have to give—a job that others don't even know to look for, let alone find.

Will it be your dream job? We hear our clients seeking a "dream job," but more often than not, it's just that, a dream, a cloud without any specific outline. Even if you know exactly what this dream job looks like, you can easily miss many other ideal opportunities around you that could lead to the dream job if you are too myopic.

Remember, your efforts will rest on the foundation of seeing yourself as a valuable product and your potential employers as potential consumers of that product. If you still need to work on your product description and placement, circle back to Chapter 3 now and redo the exercises there until you are very clear about what attributes, experiences and attitudes make up the product that is you.

The vast majority of job seekers are focused on the obvious, low hanging fruit jobs available. Sure, you can grab at those, too. But we're going to tell you how to find lucrative job opportunities most job seekers will never find—a super-secret cache of prospects.

The Low Hanging Fruit

Depending on the stage of your career, you might want to begin here. This is where 90% of your competition spends their time, but no matter. You're going to work on the obvious job openings better than everyone else. Portion a small amount of your time for the low hanging fruit. Find the jobs, submit your resume, note your submission, and move to the next steps.

Post your resume on all those publicly-facing job boards—all the ones you can find. Look on LinkedIn,

Monster, CareerBuilder, Dice—or just Google "job boards," and you'll find a seemingly endless number of them. Keep track of where and when you post your resume.

Keep yourself on top of the list and increase the likelihood that you'll actually get seen on those boards. It's simpler than you think. Every week or two, refresh the resumes you've posted on all the job boards. Your resume is heavily ranked based on a timestamp it gets when you submit or post it. So if you posted your resume two weeks ago, then everybody who has submitted a resume since then is going to be listed ahead of you in line. Your resume ends up getting stale. Keep your resume on the first couple of pages of the board resume search results by just changing a couple of words and re-saving it. Done. Now you're on top again. Even if it is a cattle-call, you might as well be prime beef.

Uncharted Territory

OK, how are you going to discover the secret stash of career opportunities your competitors miss? You already have a solid foundation with the work we've done so far. Now it's time to find your way through the jungle for the companies, and people leading you to find career opportunities—not just your next job.

Learning to Collect Data ━━━━━━━━━━━

Data offers insights and the ability to manage and focus your efforts. So a large component of the process is collecting and keeping track of valuable data about the playing field—the organizations, positions, people, influencers, hiring managers, and whoever or whatever else you deem important, thus, connecting you to your own personal end zone.

So you need some organizational tools, such as spreadsheets or a simple CRM, to help you manage this data, keep track of your action steps, check your progress, and even rank the organizations you're following and schedule meetings.

Once you've got your trusty tools, turn your attention toward positions, people, and companies.

Positions ━━━━━━━━━━━━━━━━━━━━━

What are all the job titles relating to your career search? If you're in a specialty position such as nursing, plumbing, electrical work, or landscaping, you may already have in mind a number of alternative titles that apply to you. Either way, collect all the potential position titles and potential positions you are ready or willing to grow into.

Let's see how we can expand your network. Identify the people who have the job titles you've searched for. Jump on LinkedIn, which has premium packages such as Recruiter Lite or Sales Navigator, allowing you to search through three levels of connections: geography, industry, and company size. Enter the cities or towns where you want to work, then enter the job title you're seeking. Try variations on the title, such as "copywriter" in addition to "writer." It's a fun way to gamify things, and you'll end up with a significant list of people who are already in those jobs—working for companies that employ people like you and could become great advocates for you when they hear of relevant opportunities *if* they know about you.

Companies

Next, add the companies of the people you've identified based on your list of positions and job titles from above. This will give you the ability to keep track of the internal employees and hiring managers you'll contact about opportunities. For certain professions, such as dentistry, this is a pretty straightforward process. It can be as simple as using Google or Google Maps to search for relevant dental facilities. Sometimes you can narrow titles down fairly quickly. But if you're in operations, administration, engineering, sales, marketing, or something common in many companies, plan to spend some extra time digging deep on LinkedIn and other major job sites. Glass-door can also reveal insights on a company's culture, benefits, salary ranges, and more for an enhanced, detailed picture of the potential working experience.

Rank the companies you've tagged, so that as more options open up to you, you can make informed decisions about which ones to pursue and which position you really want to nab. On the other hand, you might get some intel on a company and decide to rule them out because of some aspect that doesn't resonate with you. You could save tons of valuable time choosing to avoid a direction that won't pay off. When using a tool like Glassdoor, we'd encourage you to look for the "themes" within the reviews and not just take one person's review (positive or negative), as gospel.

Here's another tactic to find more of the less-obvious companies. Go back to your People list, and back into LinkedIn to examine their former employers. Now you've discovered uncharted territory of places that might need your skills, talents, and services and someone who can give you the inside scoop. Since these companies obviously employ people like you, they could have a potential opening currently or in the near future. Now look for people in comparable roles in these newly identified companies and add them to your list as well.

Create a list of relevant keywords to your desired position to use to search on Google, LinkedIn, or other web tools. Start with tools, certifications, associations, or systems associated with the roles and job functions you're interested in. For example, if you are a security engineer, some of the terms you might search for are security, data, network, infrastructure, CISSP, ISIS, firewalls, routers, and so forth. Coming up with keywords associated with the job function takes only a little time and will also be valuable to you as you discover groups, associations, and events with significant networking opportunities. It's also helpful for you to see what certifications and accreditations companies value.

Return to LinkedIn and find the people connected with those terms, look at the companies they work for, and see if some of those companies fit your criteria as a prospective employer. The bonus is, not only do you have a company name, but you also have the name of somebody that works there, too. Add them to your lists.

Ideally, **find five people for each company**: this could be two peers, two influencers, and at least one decision-maker/hiring manager. The influencers might include the salesperson, the office manager, a project manager, or even someone in marketing.

They're most likely people who have earned their credibility through their integrity.

Remember, many of the available jobs (and potential jobs) are at companies who are not actively advertising a potential hiring need or desire on the job boards or on LinkedIn. It doesn't mean they won't hire somebody. They simply might not have the time at the moment to take care of such matters efficiently, or they might not have the job posted yet. You want to keep them on your target list. Pursue them to find hidden jobs or create new ones out of their business needs that match up with your skills and abilities. You could be a great opportunity hire for someone.

Remember to be genuine and authentic. Showing interest in them, their careers, and companies. If someone calls you and just starts asking you a bunch of questions about your company or for a job it will get uncomfortable quickly and they'll burn you as a contact. Don't do that.

Outreach

As you build your active lists of positions, companies, and people, **start reaching out to meet over coffee or tea**. Meeting in person is way more valuable than emails or social media. If they can't meet, a video or phone call is also better than email or social media.

Face-to-face interactions offer you an opportunity to more thoroughly (but discreetly) convey your value as a product to the company or department. You'll increase the likelihood of gaining information about their company, the companies they've worked for, and the appropriate job opportunities. Keep an ear open for events to attend, groups to join and invest in, and even their guidance on or recommendations on relevant leaders and influencers.

We'll be honest: As you undertake this outreach, you'll get a whole lot of No's, a bunch of non-responders, and a smattering of Yes's. In sales and marketing, Josh has found that a 10% positive response is considered normal for cold outreach efforts. You can use this as a benchmark on the returns of your efforts. **If you reach out to 100 people, the goal is to get at least 10 people to respond**; 500 people should net 50 responses. Which would you rather have? Ten people or 50 people to network with? If you are netting at least a 10% return, you're doing well. If you find yourself getting overwhelmed with meetings, interviews, and opportunities, that's also a pretty good measure. It means you are sending out the right initial signals to prompt response. Remember that clear messaging related to your values as a product will get better response rates if you are targeting the right people.

Keep a buttoned-up approach and **prepare thoroughly for your conversation**. Go back to their LinkedIn connections and publicly-facing social media. Practice your best messaging on why and to whom you are valuable. Be ready with questions to help you learn about them and what's important to them, and with thoughts about how you may be able to add value to them. Politeness and respect are key here.

As you network with people within a company, group, or organization and you start building relationships, you'll find that peoples' perception of you grows. (It's your job to make sure it grows for the better, not worse!) To make sure they have a positive and memorable "feel" for you, make sure you invest in learning about them, what's important to them, and how you can be helpful to them. Through the conversation or at the tail end of it, sharing your value messaging and/or a little about yourself as a product is also important. If you've built a foundation for a relationship, have shared your messaging in a clear and memorable way, you'll be top of mind and have established a "trust" factor, so they'll start talking about you within the company or when they hear of a position or situation where you'd be valuable. You'll be in a spot where they've leveraged their credibility on your behalf which puts you in significantly better standing than someone else coming in cold. That's the sound of opportunity knocking.

Making the Right First Impression

Communicating with new contacts and starting conversations can be intimidating at first, here are a few examples for LinkedIn connect requests or In-Mails to get you started. You can use this type of messaging on other platforms as well.

Hi [First Name], I see we're in the same field. I'm considering pursuing employment with [Company]. Would you be open to a cup of coffee to share your experience and guidance? Thanks, [First Name]. What's your schedule like over the next few days?

[First Name], I noticed you worked (or are working) at (company). I'm considering applying for a [position title] there. Can I buy you a cup of coffee to learn more about what you like most about working there and if it would be a good career choice for me?

I came across your profile and it looks like we're both [job title]. Your company is on my target list and I'd like to learn from you what you love about the company and if you'd recommend pursuing a career there. Can I buy you a cup of coffee sometime? Thanks [Their First Name]

I noticed you worked at [Company] company as a [Job Title]. I'm considering a position there, and I'd like to get your opinion on what you liked about the company and if you'd recommend it to someone like me. Can I buy you a cup of coffee sometime to discuss? Thanks [First Name].

Simple, right? When they accept your connection on LinkedIn, send them another note to follow up with similar messaging. Even if they haven't sent you a note back along with the connection, follow up with another note saying, "Thanks for connecting on LinkedIn. I'll follow up with an email to help us actually connect."

Once someone has connected with you on LinkedIn, click on the Contact Info tab and you'll usually have access to their email address(es), Send them an email thanking them again for connecting. Include your basic messaging again, invite them for coffee, and include a calendar link (or scheduling bot) to help with scheduling. (As of this writing, x.ai and Calendly. com are tools we highly recommend.) Keep in mind that as smart as you are, you've got to make every step incredibly simple for them. This includes using a scheduling tool and identifying and suggesting a location that's convenient for them—probably one that's close to their office. Offer to meet them early or late. You'll find that if you take this approach you'll have a higher response rate, or they'll refer you to a better person to connect within their organization.

If you're writing to hiring managers or similar leaders, your message can be slightly more tailored. For example:

I found your company interesting and wanted to send a note of congratulations on your success. I'm curious if you have pain points around [Your messaging] or are looking to add this function to your team. I'd love to have a conversation with you about it. Can I buy you a cup of coffee?

I came across your company and found it compelling. Would you be up for a coffee to explore how someone with five years of experience helping companies do [what you do] might be valuable to you and your team? What's your schedule like over the next couple of weeks?

I noticed you're the recruiter at [company]. I applied for the [position]. I'm looking for a company where I can add continual value doing [add your simple messaging here]. Here's a link to my calendar [calendar link], if you'd like to schedule a quick call to expedite things. Thanks. Chat soon.

I found your ad for a [position]. It looks like you're the hiring manager. I'm looking for a company and leader where I can add value doing [insert simple messaging]. Does your schedule permit a quick discovery call to see if my skills, experience, and amazing work ethic match your needs?

When you convey your "value as a product," you never know what chord you might strike. Maybe one of their team members isn't really measuring up. Your lead might think, "Hey, Trisha Harp looks a lot more qualified and ambitious than the dude who's in the role right now. I think I'm going to talk to her, maybe swap him out." Or, maybe the leader is thinking, "Gosh, my team is overloaded right now, and I need another person in that role. But I haven't had the time to put the job description together. I should probably reach out to Trisha."

If you send out this kind of message—that you have very relevant and compelling skills and you can fulfill such-and-such needs—while 90 out of 100 might not need that right now, the remaining 10 potentially will, or they will know someone who does. You've just found 10 potential opportunities with no competition! Also keep in mind, at least 30% of the workforce is looking for a new job at any point. You can also add a little messaging in future outreach that alludes to "what happens if someone in this role leaves?" Fear is a heck of a motivator.

Never pummel people with your history, your skills, or your accomplishments early in the process. Don't bore them with news about your company. Don't talk about me-me-me. Don't give a sales spiel—start a conversation. Ask about pain points or goals they're trying to accomplish that are relevant to your skills and experience. They get 50 resumes a day. Why should they talk to you? Ask compelling questions to get people interested. Focus on their needs and goals—not what you want, need, think, or feel.

Following Up

After sending out a bazillion copies of their resumes to postings on job boards, many people often think that their work is done, and it's just a matter of waiting for responses and landing that dream job. But as we know, everyone out there is busy and overwhelmed with competing priorities. And now they have a massive number of resumes to sort through as a response to their job post. At this point, you are just another resume they have to review.

But you're already doing several things very differently. You're being active, proactive, and reactive—you're working a list of 500 companies, making connections, having coffee with new and existing contacts, finding multiple entry approaches, and engaging with people in these companies that can refer and recommend you. You are approaching all arising opportunities in ways that your competition can't and won't even think of. You'll have peers and influencers recommending you for the positions you've applied to. Who do you think hiring managers are most likely to invest time in first? One of the many that have applied, or the one that their team keeps recommending to them? Sure, it's a little more work, but the returns are much greater.

Remember, one email or one outreach falls flat in today's marketplace; you'll end up missing a majority of the opportunities that could be great matches for you and the companies. If they don't respond, don't complain. Keep at it. When they do respond, execute on your plan, have your responses and follow-up ready. Set a reminder for a follow-up. Be ready to mention the people who've referred you to them, and be prepared with all the information you've gathered. Have a great answer as to why you are a great fit for them based on the information you've learned from the relevant contacts you've connected and met with.

A mix of LinkedIn messages, emails, calls, text messages, coffee/lunch, with contacts will net you a much better result than just a single application with a resume to a post or a single email hoping for a response. Put yourself in the hiring manager's shoes. They are often completely overwhelmed with their job and their team, plus they have to handle hiring on top of everything else. When they make a bad hiring decision, it ends up having a negative effect on them and the whole team. When they make a good hiring decision, the team prospers. It can be really stressful for them. Make it easy for them to see you as someone who's a great hiring decision.

Sweetening the Pot

Once you've spent a little time getting to know someone, and you feel confident that they see you as credible, ask them if they have a company referral program. They could earn a little money while passing along your name to a manager or HR. Now you aren't just a new contact, you are someone who could have a significant check attached. Now you have a champion in the organization working for you.

Making Social Media a Productive Tool

We've found that LinkedIn, Facebook, Instagram, Twitter, and other social media sites and apps can work to your job-search advantage. But as you know, social media can also suck you in and spit you out several hours later, your head spinning. We recommend limiting yourself to 45 minutes or less of "fun" social media time. If you constantly find yourself going past this time allotment, set an alarm. Then stop when the alarm goes off!

Social media can lead you to valuable information, networking opportunities, relevant events, conferences, communities, and people to invest in and grow with. It can also be a place for you to post and share valuable information from your experience that others can learn from.

Start by following and getting active on the social media platforms of your targeted companies. One might be more active on Facebook; another may keep strictly to LinkedIn. Follow their hiring managers and influencers and keep an eye out for posts on open positions or questions relevant to your experience and ability. Like and comment (thoughtfully and carefully) on their posts.

Look for interesting posts, articles, blogs, and white papers that align with the interests of your intended audience. Share relevant posts with your contacts on social media, which can be a very productive relationship-building tool. You gain credibility among prospective employers, who see how you're active and engaged in your desired profession.

> Josh knew an interior designer (let's call him Chad) who was amazing and wanted to get into movie set design. In addition to applying for positions he found, Chad began following and attending everything related to movie sets. He'd show up at the relevant conferences and conventions and events. Chad had never done a freaking movie set in his life, yet he got hired by a studio to do a set for a movie, which led to another, then another, and eventually led to his landing a contract as a head set designer within three years. Chad was used to making about $90,000 as an interior designer, and then, all of a sudden, he had a $300k position with million-dollar budgets. He was traveling all over the world doing set design and working with some of the most incredible people in the entertainment world. Josh hates Chad. :)

Leave positive comments on other posts, maybe even asking if your contacts have time for a brief discussion on the topic. The more positive touchpoints you can have with someone or within a community—even if it's just clicking the "Like" button on a post—the more credibility you build and the more likely it is that people will respond to you directly.

Remember, you're not just building a digital database of people and companies and jobs. You're engaging with others to convey your capability and your value.

Easing into Events

Remember Angie's story from Chapter 1? She had the self-confidence to land multiple job offers from a single event during a bad time in the economy. Plenty of us, however, are still freaked out by walking into a room full of people we don't know. Our faces flush, our palms sweat, and our hearts start beating like crazy.

Now picture yourself going into the same room confident in your abilities, heavily armed with your value statements and product messaging that revolves around why and where you are valuable. And you have a clearly prescribed mission: to meet as many people as you can by doing the same thing over and over again. This is all you need to do:

1. Extend out your hand.
2. Introduce yourself and ask a couple of questions about them and what they do.
3. Offer up the messaging about your value that you prepared.
4. Exchange cards and say you'll follow up.

5. Walk to the next person and repeat steps 1–4.
6. Actually, really, and truly: follow up. Send each person a note expressing gratitude for meeting them and invite them for coffee. If they haven't responded within three days, again, take a deep breath, get in the right headspace, follow up with a phone call.

As you do this a few times, it gets easier and easier, especially if you focus on discovery and what you have to offer people that will bring value to them or someone they know. And you'll fare even better by focusing on how you can help each other—not a specific job offer.

Remember, it takes time to build momentum as you start to make connections, find new paths to travel, meet new people, get your name out there, and understand more and more about how you can be of value and service to the right company.

In the next chapter, we'll give you power lessons on working smart, avoiding pitfalls, getting out of your own way, and other tips on making the ride easier, more rewarding, and ultimately successful.

NOTES

_____

_____

_____

_____

_____

_____

_____

_____

_____

_____

_____

_____

_____

_____

_____

_____

_____

_____

_____

_____

_____

_____

_____

_____

_____
_____
_____
_____
_____
_____
_____
_____
_____
_____
_____
_____
_____
_____
_____
_____
_____
_____
_____
_____
_____
_____
_____
_____
_____
_____
_____
_____

CHAPTER 7:

Powering Up and Fine Tuning

Goals keep you focused and motivated, they give structure to your work, and they make it possible to measure and monitor your success. They also help keep you honest with your progress and give you little successes to celebrate along the way. Feel free to start out by setting your goals a little lower until you get more into the groove of your search. Then you can crank them up. In other words, it's okay to underachieve in the beginning. Just remember, you have to keep raising the bar.

G-O-A-L

Trish spent the better part of her early career starting and running programs for individuals with developmental disabilities. While she enjoyed her work, she knew it wasn't what she wanted to do for the rest of her life. She was married. Life was starting to get more complicated as her responsibility was no longer just to herself. Since childhood, her gut had always drawn her toward helping people to better themselves, but she really wanted to be there for her peers in more of an entrepreneurial way. During an angst-ridden conversation with her husband, she expressed how she desperately wanted to go back to school to achieve her goals. But how? She and her husband went through a process she designed called G-O-A-L to figure out how to:

- overcome challenges of studying for the GRE
- take the dreaded test
- identify the right program to apply for
- network with "champions" who could help get her into her program of choice
- take an "education leave of absence" from her job

- ensure they had enough capital in their start-up so she could work while also going to school

GOAL	Objective the person wants to reach – be sure the goal is clear.	Questions to ask:	What specifically do you want to accomplish?	When do you want to have this done?
OBSTACLES	Determine a realistic starting point and identify obstacles.	Questions to ask:	What are your current obstacles?	What have you already done to start accomplishing this goal?
ANSWERS	Develop at least 5 potential solutions. Be creative; you have options.	Questions to ask:	If you had unlimited resources and knew you couldn't fail, what would you try?	What have you seen others do that might work for you? Are there other people or resources you could tap?
LEAN-IN	Turn your preferred solution into actionable steps.	Questions to ask:	What steps could you take this week toward your goal?	On a scale of 1 – 10 how likely are you to take that step in the time you allotted? What obstacles can you cut out?

© Harp Family Institute 2020

Any goal worth having comes with obstacles, says Trish, pointing to the O in GOAL. As a result of this discussion, they ended up with a one-word family motto: "choices." "We are never stuck," she says. "We *always* have options, no matter how hard they are to uncover."

Here are some questions to ask yourself to get started with goals. They're not too heavy-handed to overburden you, yet they're incisive enough to keep you on track and moving forward.

Starter Goals

- How many opportunities am I going to commit to finding and applying for each day, each week, and each month?
- How many networking meetings am I going to commit to scheduling and attending each week? Each month?
- How many interviews am I going to aim for per month?
- How many potential employers am I committed to uncovering and connecting with daily, weekly, and monthly?
- How many relevant groups, networking events, or industry events will I commit to attending on a monthly basis?

If you aren't currently working, we'd suggest aiming to schedule at least five meetings or networking events per week to start. If you are working, set the goals to the level just beyond what's comfortable. If you're having to book things out a couple of weeks because you have too many people to meet with, it's a good sign; you should feel good about your progress because you're booked. Again, limit yourself to investing and participating in what adds the most potential value to your process.

Nicole started her career in consulting. Nicole is a 9-foot tall bulletproof superhero who resides in a 5'2", 110-lb frame—she's fierce. After going unnoticed for a while, keeping her head down, Nicole started out-producing her peers. At her first annual review, she got great marks and a reasonable raise. At the end of the review meeting, she thanked her boss and asked for 10% more. He was stunned. Before he could say anything she hit him with her accomplishments; how she was valuable to the team; and the above and beyond effort she'd invested. She'd never missed a deadline, complained, or asked for anything, and would appreciate his support in fairly compensating her for her continued efforts and helping her continue to be motivated to outperform her peers. She got the 10%.

This isn't the end of the story. A week later Nicole set a meeting with her boss and shared with him what she wanted to accomplish over the next year to make sure it was aligned with his needs and goals. Indeed it did. She then sucker-punched him by asking him this amazing question: "If we can accomplish all of this together, can I continue to have your support by promoting me to manager and adjusting my salary to $XXX?" She'd done her homework, she knew the salary bands, she asked for something just north of appropriate, and then

> sat there staring at her boss until he responded. Guess
> what he said?

It's normal to have a slower pace when you start but remember the law of momentum. Objects in motion tend to stay in motion, and objects at rest tend to stay at rest. The momentum you build will increase the volume of connections, meetings, and opportunities. Keep building on your activity level and flexing your communication and networking muscles. Believing in yourself and your value will not only give you confidence, but it will also increase the confidence that others have in you, your abilities, and your value. Remember: if you want to get comfortable with doing something that seems hard, you have to get uncomfortable with it first.

Avoid the Rabbit Holes

We can "save" time, "spend" time, "waste" time, and even "buy" time, just as we can with money. Time is a valuable but limited resource, so you want to be smart about how you manage, invest in, and spend it. It's shocking to us how many people (ourselves included) can be sucked down the rabbit hole of distraction, starting with the online world.

As you research companies and collect contacts, stay intentional and purposeful. Look for the traits we discussed earlier. Your cadence will have a huge impact on your success. Online productivity trackers can help you gauge how much time to spend on each part of the process.

If you just spent an hour on something and you have nothing to show for it, you've wasted each one of those 60 minutes when you could have been making serious progress on your search. Next time, find and record at least five opportunities to connect, apply, or inquire. The goal is to accumulate opportunities as you continue to refine your process.

Refine Your Online Presence

You show up on time for meetings, well-dressed, sharp, and prepared. So why does your reflection seem to be missing, sloppy, confused, and unprepared?

We're talking about your online presence here, and you have a far lower probability of getting the job you most want if you fail to get this right.

Having a polished image online is critically important to achieving your goals. Assume that every potential employer or contact will see what you put online (even if you think it's private). Slip-ups from the past, whether they're job skirmishes or questionable photos, are a one-way, slippery slope to the bottom of the hiring bucket. You're fighting for survival with those crabs we discussed earlier. So scrub the grimy stuff or start clean if you need to.

Look at your online profiles from the perspective of your future employer. As a hiring manager, would you employ someone with racially-charged, sexist, demeaning, angry, or derogatory online posts? What about someone who's been pestering others with emotionally charged comments? Nope! They have their teams and their companies to protect, and there's no room whatsoever for a sketchy hire.

So, review your social media and LinkedIn content and make sure the writing is clean, well-written, thoughtful, and compelling. Be sure to include success stories that demonstrate your abilities and accomplishments. Describe how and where you can be most helpful to companies. Show your engagement by commenting on interesting and compelling posts, professionally and personally. Repost interesting or inspiring articles. Everything about you that's publicly-facing tells people about who you are.

Also, this one may seem a little obvious, but smile for your profile pictures.

Make the Most of Networking Meetings

Yes, we've discussed this topic before, but here's your final checklist before a networking meeting, which can be like a dress rehearsal for showtime: the interview (which we'll discuss in Chapter 8).

Messaging. Before your meeting, review your notes, thoughts, and messaging about who you are as a product. Memorizing a line or two is encouraged. Try to be as concise as you can so you don't babble.

Networking. You could end up face to face and connect to other potential employers. Come to the meeting with a list of the companies and potential relationships you were able to find on their LinkedIn or social media profiles.

Objectives. The predominant objective is to build relationships. Next is to network, convey your messaging, and open opportunities for your career. What will accomplish those goals? First: spending time inquiring about them and the company's needs. Second: discussing how you can be helpful to them or mentioning people you know that might be good resources for them. And last: asking for their help in your career search. Be ready to share your lists of people and companies with whom you know they are connected. Ask them for their thoughts and opinions around working with them, and ask if they'd be willing to make an introduction.

Attitude. You want to come across as genuine, enthusiastic, positive, appreciative, capable, confident, forward-looking—and humble. The goal is for them to leave with nothing but positive feelings about you and to be memorable. Remember that how you say something is at least as important as what you say. Avoid, like the plague, any expressions of negativity, woundedness, anger, frustration, neediness, fear, obsession, indignance, arrogance, bigotry, disingenuousness, etc. After all, if you met two different people who were asking you for help with networking, one had a positive attitude and the other had a negative attitude, who would you be more inclined to help? It's profound how important and influential the energy you bring to a meeting can be.

One of Trisha's favorite quotes is from Barbara Johnson: "Attitude is the mind's paintbrush; it can color any situation," Approaching challenges with a positive attitude has opened some incredible doors for her throughout the years. People naturally prefer to be around a Pooh, a Tigger, and a Rabbit vs. an Eeyore.

What to Share

Depending on your relationship, this might be:

- What you're trying to accomplish through networking
- Where and how you are of value to an organization
- A list of potential connections they may have
- A list of contacts or companies from your research where they have connections or potential insights
- Your personal brand that makes it simple for them to introduce you to others (one or two sentences summarizing your value, i.e., your elevator pitch)

Order of Business. Every meeting is different, but here's a rough timeline to keep you on track:

- Take about 5–10 minutes for small talk. The weather, the drive, family, friends, things happening in the community or industry, the day, etc.
- Expect to spend about 10–15 minutes asking them questions about their job, their company, an open position, or whatever may be

important to them—and then listen to their answers. Listen for how you can be helpful to them and who you might connect them with in order to help them accomplish, solve, or overcome something important or valuable to them.

- Take only 3–5 minutes to share your message that conveys you as a product and how you might be helpful to them.

- Take about 10 minutes to ask if they'd be willing to help you with introductions or networking and talking about intros and contacts where you can add value. (More about this below.)

- Finally, take a few minutes to wrap up the conversation. Go over the ways you've agreed to be helpful to each other through introductions, knowledge share, and networking. Review the action items for both of you and thank them profusely for their time and help.

Once you have someone engaged with a clear understanding of where and how you are valuable, you'll find networking gets much easier. This is simply because you've done such a good job of articulating your messaging. Ask them if they'd be open to helping you network to identify the right opportunities and people to connect with.

Trish was working with a coaching client, Jim, practicing how to structure his responses to a variety of questions. When he first came to Trish, he was stiff, awkward and framed his answers in a defensive, self-serving manner. As more of a technically minded individual, he didn't put much credence on warm-fuzzy ways of communicating but was finding he kept hitting a brick wall at work. Trish worked with him to express the same thoughts, but with some humor, smiles, and warmth. She also helped him shift his "I" talk into "we" and "you" talk. He called Trish after the meeting to tell her how much he crushed it! He shared how much he had learned during their sessions, not only about how to position things during that particular meeting but also how to engage more effectively with friends, family, and coworkers.

Widen (or Narrow) Your Scope

By now in your job-search process, chances are you've considered other opportunities outside of one particular title. It's time, though, to review that scope before it's too late and you land in a role not really meant for you. Just because you've been in Human Resources for most of your career doesn't mean you have to stay there. You might have great people skills that are equally applicable in a different department. If you're an auto mechanic, think about looking for jobs for airplane mechanics, boat mechanics, or even a trainer.

Remember that when companies are short on talent, they're often more generous with training—more willing to invest in people who don't have the full skill set but who demonstrate that they'll work hard and smart. You might be able to get the training you need to make the transition and find yourself in a very rewarding new environment with amazing growth potential.

And the same is also true when you narrow down your position to a specialty. For example, maybe you're experienced in general paralegal, but you want to target real estate law. Maybe you're a nurse who wants to focus in geriatric care. Or maybe you're a marketing consultant who wants to land in a specialty such as social media. The key is to talk with your TAB (Trusted Advisory Board) about it so they can help you hone your messaging and approach.

Own Your Emotional Baggage

You can't walk into a networking meeting and be at your best if you have negative emotional or psychological issues robbing you of the ability to react and interact in a healthy, productive manner. You could offset your entire career trajectory if you hold onto traumas, wounds, fears, and disappointments from the past and refuse to deal with them or invest in healing them. If your negative emotions continue to demand your attention or sap your energy, you will find it harder to effectively define yourself, your value, and your sense of being a product in your industry, let alone to have a bright, confident, and focused conversation.

If you have some emotional issues dragging you down or impeding your ability to be your best—and you really do want to land a great job—you have two choices: find a way to deal with it, or package it neatly so it doesn't stink. Don't let something or someone who's stolen from you in the past rob you of an amazing future.

Whatever your story is, imagine it all was the first part of someone else's movie. Create an outline for the movie, complete with a beginning, middle, and an end. You already know the beginning, and some of the middle, so now it's time to focus on the rest of the story. What's the next part of the movie where the hero overcomes what's in the past and does something amazing to turn it all around? What impact did the past experience have on them that pushed them to be more successful than they thought they could ever be? What did they learn from that experience that allowed them to help someone else? Remember that you are the writer of your own story. Don't let the story write you. How does the story end? The facts are still just the facts. What you do with them, whether or not you let them push you down, and how you stand on them to raise yourself up is your choice. Leaders want people who build themselves up, not someone who is constantly feeling pushed down.

A sense of gratitude, while truly beneficial to your own emotional health, will also come across very well in your messaging. Be able to communicate what you're thankful for and why you're thankful. It comes across with much more genuineness than the standard facts-only answers. Here's a sample note you can write to yourself:

"I was in a rough situation, and it was really challenging when I was in the middle of it; but, I'm really thankful for the experience now because I met these three people out of it. You know we managed to figure out how to actually do X and Y successfully. We found out that if we are going down that path, it would have been a lot more painful than if we'd stopped at that point. So, I'm really, really thankful for what I learned and the people

I met. Because of that experience, I created a bond with some people that I'll have for the rest of my life."

Here are some other ways to frame some of the challenging chapters of your life when asked about them:

- I'm proud of how I handled it and thankful for what I have learned.
- I learned a lot about my character through this experience and am thankful for the experience and the relationships that came from it.
- Nobody likes losing, but this was just a battle, not the war.
- It wasn't a failure—just a tough way for me to learn important lessons.
- I worked with some amazing people who have helped me learn that the game's not over until we win.
- I got all my teeth knocked out, but I picked 'em all up and smiled. While I couldn't change the situation, I did have a say in how we handled it and reacted to it!
- [Bleep] you for asking that!!! (Obviously, we are kidding here, though we realize this is

sometimes the desired response, so we added it in for some comic relief!)

By now, you've hopefully pushed down on that gas pedal, have scrubbed your forward-facing persona and are on a roll with your meetings and connections. The final step is to learn what it takes to set yourself up for a winning interview. It takes the right kind of preparation, a willingness to practice ahead of time, and the right mindset going in. For best results, learn how to engage your interviewer in a dialog, rather than sit there passively answering questions. All of that awaits you in Chapter 8.

NOTES

_____
_____
_____
_____
_____
_____
_____
_____
_____
_____
_____

_____

_____

_____

_____

_____

_____

_____

_____

_____

_____

_____

_____

_____

_____

_____

_____

_____

_____

_____

_____

_____

CHAPTER 8:

Inside the Interview

Finally. You've arrived at the door. Now it's time to go through the door.

To get into interview mode, you're going to have to switch gears a bit. So far, your process of finding and landing a career has been mostly an isolated exercise, data-driven, numbers-driven, and under your control. Now it's time to get out from behind your desk and interact with people who can hire you and make an impact on the course of your career. This means: knowing what mindset to bring with you, how you want to present yourself, how you're going to interact, and how you're going to prepare.

Prepare, Prepare, Prepare

"By failing to prepare, you are preparing to fail," said Ben Franklin. You simply must prepare for the interview by anticipating questions; reviewing the interviewer's profiles; knowing the company's offerings, value, profile, team, metrics, and motivations; feeling comfortable with how you're presenting yourself; and preparing for the unexpected. All these will make it so much faster, easier, and more enjoyable for your interviewer to see that you are the one for the job. Preparing allows you to be more genuine and collaborative in an interview because you can focus on the conversation, rather than trying to figure things out on the fly.

In fact, walking into the interview, having obviously prepared for it, communicates something very positive all by itself.

Practice, Practice, Practice

If you want to run a marathon, you don't just show up that day and start running. Ouch. It's the same thing with interviewing. When you train for them, interviews should no longer be painful.

Let's say the interviewer asks you a tough question. The worst thing you can do is make up something meaningless on the spot, say something cute, or even pivot to another topic without actually answering the question. Just say you don't know the answer, or you need a little more context to relate it to their specific needs or pain points. You can also share how you'd go about finding the answer or the best solution.

But, luckily, you've done your research, you know your "audience," and you have a clearer idea of what they are seeking in a candidate, the culture they want people to fit into, their goals, and how you can help them meet those goals. You have the foundation for answering virtually any question thrown at you. But to really bring your "A" game, you need to work and practice with the types of questions your interviewer will probably ask you:

1. Tell me about yourself.
2. Why do you want this job?
3. Why should we hire you?
4. What is your greatest strength? Weakness?
5. Why do you want to leave (or have you left) your current job?
6. What are your salary expectations?
7. How do you handle stress or pressure?
8. Describe a difficult work situation or project and how you overcame it.

9. What are your goals for the future?
10. Why are you the best person for the job?
11. What makes you stand out against the competition?
12. Give an example of how you work well with others.
13. How do you handle conflict?
14. Tell me about a situation where you've failed?
15. What are you proudest of professionally?
16. What's your biggest accomplishment?
17. What are you doing to actively invest in yourself and your career?
18. What is the answer to the ultimate question?

While this is far from a complete list, spend time with each question and craft several talking points for your responses. Since you've gone through the whole process of identifying yourself as a product and understanding how your value relates to a company's potential goals, needs, or pain points, bring those perspectives into your responses. That's your messaging. While it won't be right for every situation, it'll resonate with the right people and opportunities. As you practice, refer to your notes from your work in previous chapters to inspire your ideas. Remember, you are searching for the right job. Not just any job.

Ask your TAB, your family, your friends, or even your dog to give you mock interviews. If their feedback is solid (leaving out the dog here), then fold in their suggestions to your response and see if it sharpens your answer. You may be surprised how natural and impactful it feels to rephrase an answer using their suggestions.

Listening for Unspoken Cues

As we've discussed before, you can also learn what people are saying with their body language and facial expressions. This can be a huge differentiator. When you see a change in their body language or expression, you can tell if they're leaning into your answers and questions or pulling away from them. This then allows you to ask follow-up questions that show a high E.Q. and ability to communicate that most people miss.

The more you practice with potential interview questions, the more comfortable you'll be as you sit and talk with your interviewer, and the more confident you'll come across. The more it will feel like a collaboration instead of an interview. So, practice, practice, practice.

Choose the Right Mindset

The key here is to enter the interview with a collaborative mindset, instead of a confrontational mindset.

You've done your research about the company, and you know yourself as a product—two things that most other candidates won't have done. That means you better know how you and the company could match up—and why. Armed with those insights, you want to walk into the interview intending to have a conversation—a dialog—and create a collaboration. Go in with the mindset that the purpose of the interview is to have a real, genuine, open conversation around whether the job is a good match for you and for them. Your intention is to explore the job, your opportunity to grow, the conditions, and the possibilities together—to understand each other better and see if there's a mutually beneficial relationship in your futures. Instead of sitting there trying to "get" a job, you're putting your heads together to discuss and explore how much you can contribute to the company and decide if it's a place where you can thrive, grow, and add meaningful value, too.

We all come to the table with our own thoughts, opinions, and beliefs. Some of these are ingrained and come from our core belief system, some have developed over years of life and our experiences. Regardless of what you are coming to the table believing, it's important to clear your mind, shake off your emotional baggage, and attempt to bring an open mind. Recognizing that everyone sitting around the table all brings preconceived beliefs will help you, as an individual, make the conscious choice, to come with a collaborative mindset instead of a confrontational one. If each person took charge of approaching conversations as a member of a team vs as an individual with an agenda item to push forward, just imagine the collaboration that could transpire. Instead, many of us are so used to fighting for what we want, believe and feel, that over the years, it's hard not to lose the ability to collaborate effectively and thus, often get nothing of consequence accomplished. — Trish

Conflict mentalities keep people apart; collaboration mentalities bring people together. Don't let your insecurities, nervousness, or even excitement allow you to contribute to anything confrontational.

If the interviewer comes across like they are in a confrontational mindset, you have a choice to play into that, or you can treat it as an opportunity to create a collaboration. If you can't get to the point where you are having a conversation that's comfortable, you have to ask yourself if there's potential for things to get more comfortable as you get to know each other and work together. If there is, then keep exploring the opportunity. If there isn't, they may not be someone you want to be working for in the long term.

Your Questions

Because you're collaborating, both of you will be asking questions. Your thought process and approach should be more like a consultant than an applicant. Your premise is that the two of you are a team already, and you're figuring out how working together can help to alleviate some of the company's pain points and help further its goals. Your attitude is: "Tell me what your needs are, and then let's see if my strengths and the things that I'm passionate about can help you with them." Or: "I want to understand the pain points of this team and discover how I can help you reduce them as well as the stress around them. I'm really good at doing that. Here's how. Here's why I'm valuable."

You may need to assert yourself a little more than you're used to in interviews by asking discovery or clarifying questions. Demonstrate that you're informed, inquisitive, and motivated. For example: "I read that the company is experiencing X, and I'm wondering if there's a pain point around (that topic) that this job would directly address. I'd like to understand exactly how I can be of most help to reach those goals."

Here are some questions to help you shine:

- Why is this position open?
- What other areas and people will the person in this role need to work with?
- What's the impact if someone in this role fails to perform?
- Can you tell me the biggest challenge you're trying to solve right now?
- Can you tell me about the team and how they're operating right now?
- Why didn't the person previously in this position work out? What needs to improve or change for future success in this role?
- What does the team love most about working here?
- What do you want to accomplish with your department?
- How can I be most valuable in this role to you, the team, and the company?

- I want to make sure I'm a good fit for you, the team, and the company. What stood out about me from my resume?

When you lean in, are genuine, and ask the right questions, you show you're interested, that you want to contribute, and that you're energized about the job and the company. Even if you're an introvert, you can ask great questions that show you're excited. Just remember to stay aware and attuned with your interviewer and how they're responding to you. Ask questions that show that you're attuned to them. "Can you help me understand that a little bit more?" This immediately creates an opportunity for collaboration instead of conflict. It turns you into an ally rather than an adversary. And that is to everyone's advantage.

Walking in with a spirit of collaboration and the intention of building rapport will work to your advantage. So smile—with a genuine, look-them-in-the-eyes smile. Some people go into interviews and don't smile even once—and it's usually not because they don't smile at all. They're just so nervous that they don't smile. Don't let that be you.

Tough Questions

Now you're in an interview, and a tough question hits you. The best way to answer it is with authenticity and eye contact. Don't apologize. Simply be honest about your ability to answer the question and if you don't know the answer, tell them how you would go about solving or resolving it. For example: "I'm not sure I have an answer for that one right now, but I can tell you how I'd go about finding a solution for it. I'd want to consult with X first, and then I'd want to find out how things have worked in the past. I'd want to engage people that have the necessary experience or knowledge to make sure I'm headed in the right direction. That way, I make sure I'm making the best possible decisions."

Employers don't want someone who's bullsh&^%ing them or claiming to be able to get results by relying on their gut feelings. Everyone runs into gaps in their experience and current abilities. Telling your interviewer how you would bridge that gap can make a bigger impression than many other answers. Good leaders want good decision-makers on their teams.

You Are Indiana Jones

You know, Indiana Jones could have just gone home.

He could have turned around, tossed the whip and the gun, and said to his monkey companion, "You know, I don't want to deal with this crap anymore. I'm going home."

But he didn't. He didn't quit. He pushed through everything and did what people didn't expect. And he got the girl, earned some gold, and saved the Holy Grail.

So be like Indiana Jones. (If you don't know who Indiana Jones is, I'd strongly encourage you to watch the 1981 movie *Indiana Jones and the Raiders of the Lost Ark*.)

Think of your career as an adventure. Let yourself get excited about it. What's around the next corner for you? A cliff, a beautiful vista, a bag of gold, the best job ever? It might not be easy, but it should be very rewarding.

While you're at it, let your excitement show and grow. Be excited about the journey you're on and let it show in your eyes, your voice, and your smile, whether you're meeting in person or in a video interview. People are more likely to hire you if they see you're in motion, moving toward an amazing future. They'll want to be part of your adventure.

And the best way for them to do that is to hire you.

NOTES

_____

_____

_____

_____

_____

_____

_____

_____

_____

_____

_____

_____

_____

_____

_____

_____

_____

_____

_____

_____
_____
_____
_____
_____
_____
_____
_____
_____
_____
_____
_____
_____
_____
_____
_____
_____
_____
_____
_____
_____
_____
_____
_____

_____

_____

_____

_____

_____

_____

_____

_____

_____

_____

_____

_____

_____

_____

_____

_____

_____

_____

_____

_____

_____

_____

_____

_____

_____

ACKNOWLEDGMENTS

We would like to thank the following people for helping us along our journey.

We would like to acknowledge Diane Eaton, who helped organize and focus our material. Nick Pavlidis and especially Sarah Tuff Dunn with Authority Ghostwriting who were invaluable in leveraging their experience to enhance this book from good to great. Thank you, Gary Markle, for inspiring Josh to push forward and for asking him great questions along the way to make sure he was thinking about this from the business side of writing a book. Thank you, Tommy Breedlove for inspiring Josh, making the time to help keep him focus on the right things, and Chris Tuff for sharing all of his experience around writing a book, helping us make good decisions, and avoiding the bad ones. Thank you to Bonnie Rausch, Jim Howard and David Hancock of Morgan James Publishing for carrying us over the finish line! We humbly thank all of you knowing that this book would never have happened without you.

We would like to acknowledge that this isn't a complete work. There will always be new things, techniques, perspectives, and technology that will shape how we react and interact. Our hope is that through this book, your career will move further faster and be more rewarding in every measurable way.

ABOUT THE AUTHORS

Josh McAfee is a husband with a very patient wife, and a new father who knows he's in over his head. He's spent more than 26 years in the recruiting and coaching world working with and placing thousands of leaders, sales, and tech savvy people with some amazing companies. He founded, build, and sold a national tech staffing company bases Atlanta, and has helped hundreds of companies and leaders grow their teams with the right people to have a positive impact on their products, culture, and ultimately their customers. In his personal life, he invests his time in helping people and bringing them together. His community work includes North Point Community Church in Atlanta, Jars of Clay Mission in south Atlanta, and 410 Bridge (humanitarian work in Africa and Haiti). Josh also volunteers for the Georgia Aquarium on fundraising and creating irresistible events driving community involvement and awareness.

Josh spent 6 years in the youth ministry with Peachtree Presbyterian Church in Atlanta, sat on several society boards with the Technology Association of Georgia (TAG), and served in leadership with Atlanta's High Tech Ministries and Ambassadors program.

To relax and recharge Josh seeks out adventures. Whether it's wakeboarding, surfing, racing cars and karts, martial arts, kayaking, driving his wife crazy, rappelling, traveling, getting into trouble, getting out of trouble, or just sitting on the dock with his feet in the water, Josh knows that the life and the time we have is a gift that should not be wasted. We need to measure up to what we're made to be, invest in the things and people God puts in our paths, and also enjoy what we're blessed with.

***

Trisha Harp, M.S., C.P.C., is an entrepreneur, researcher, author, and coach. She has spent the past two decades working with couples, teams, and individuals on mastering advanced communication techniques with the goal of strengthening their relationships both at home and at the office through her company, The Harp Family Institute.

After going through her own "why until you cry" experience, Trisha discovered her passion stems from the desire to help adults sort through their hang-ups so they will ultimately do a better job with their own children. (A desire which originated with helping friends deal with their struggles during her formative school years).

Over the years, Trisha's extensive proprietary research has been effective and helpful to not just entrepreneurs, but the general population as well. To date, Trisha has written five books and is in the process of writing three more. She has been featured in *Inc.* Magazine, *Entrepreneur.com*, *Forbes.com*, *Medium*, *Women 2.0*, and the *Wall Street Journal*.

In her free time, Trisha enjoys playing tennis, art & photography, and SCUBA diving with her husband and kids on the island of Bonaire.

A free ebook edition is available with the purchase of this book.

To claim your free ebook edition:

1. Visit MorganJamesBOGO.com
2. Sign your name CLEARLY in the space
3. Complete the form and submit a photo of the entire copyright page
4. You or your friend can download the ebook to your preferred device

A **FREE** ebook edition is available for you or a friend with the purchase of this print book.

CLEARLY SIGN YOUR NAME ABOVE

Instructions to claim your free ebook edition:
1. Visit MorganJamesBOGO.com
2. Sign your name CLEARLY in the space above
3. Complete the form and submit a photo of this entire page
4. You or your friend can download the ebook to your preferred device

Print & Digital Together Forever.

Snap a photo

Free ebook

Read anywhere